Plain Talk

Contributed by White County Historical Society

Plain Talk

Edited by
Carol Burke

Purdue University Press
West Lafayette, Indiana

Library of Congress Card Catalog Number 82-81678
International Standard Book Number 0-911198-67-9
Printed in the United States of America

Table of Contents

Acknowledgments

I would first like to thank the people who gave generously of their stories. Without their keen memories and lively imaginations this book would not exist. I am grateful to Tri-County superintendent Charles Downing and to principals Nile Fox and Bill Isaacs who supported this project. I owe a special debt to Joy Seybold, Jeannie French, and Chuck Hintzman of the English department who patiently trained their students to interview and who ceaselessly listened to tapes. I would also like to thank Natalie Leimkuhler whose careful work in the darkroom produced this book's illustrations. My gratitude, too, to Florence Bowman, Jerry Cook, and Dick Wheeler, whose knowledge of the area I relied on heavily.

Many people cheerfully lent a hand with transcription and cataloging; among them were Charlene Martin, Sherri Peck, Sandra Longest, Ellen Goad, Lisa Farney, Rhonda Stempkowski, Julie Bowers, and Kim Holder. Charleen Bahler generously volunteered her time to type the manuscript. My thanks to Marilyn Abbott, curator of the White County Historical Society, who helped us in our search for old photographs.

Without the financial support of the Indiana Arts Commission and the cooperation of the Tri-County School Corporation this project would not have been possible.

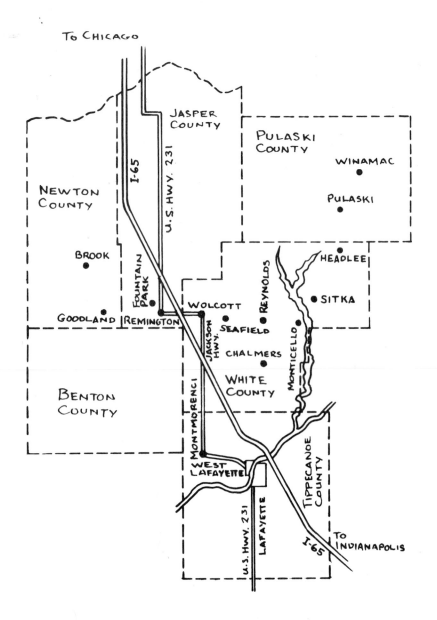

Indiana Counties Where *Plain Talk* Originated

Introduction

This is a collection of reminiscences and stories gathered in tape-recorded interviews with residents of north-central Indiana, most of whom farm or belong to families who have farmed the black soil of White, Jasper, and Benton counties. This land, reclaimed from bogs, once supported diverse crops and livestock. Now most of the cattle, the wheat, and the oats are gone; the traveler who passes through on I-65, which intersects these rich counties, can see at one time all the variety there is to see — thousands of acres devoted to the efficient, profitable production of soybeans and corn. By nature a conservative people, these farmers and sons of farmers have experienced enormous changes in agriculture during their lifetimes — changes that have brought with them a financial prosperity and security unknown to previous generations but that have also imposed a perspective, part business-like, part-scientific, alien to the past and perhaps to the land itself. The weather is still the farmer's most benevolent friend as well as his cruelest foe; but the weather now has formidable rivals for preeminence in the lobbies of Congress, the laboratories of the universities, and the floors of the exchanges in Chicago and New York. No matter how much he has conserved, no matter how much he owns, no farmer in these counties can hope any longer to live solely off the land.

In their stories, the participants in this project recall a time when farm families were, of necessity, closer to the land: when the weather was forecast by the signs, when there was no insurance for crops. Longtime residents of communities like Wolcott, Remington, Reynolds, Chalmers, Brookston, and Monon shared with us stories of little money and much work, of school pranks, of chivarees, of dates on bobsleds, of their childhoods and their adult working lives. The value of these selections lies not in their uniqueness but in the imaginative representation of common experiences and shared belief—a regional lore. By preserving in narrative the often humorous, sometimes tragic events and impressions of the past, a people creates its own image, looks at itself, and realizes its own identity.

In an effort to preserve the oral quality of these stories, we have transcribed them word for word from the taped interviews. The selections here represent only a small portion of the stories collected in the over two hundred interviews in the last three years. High school sophomores and juniors conducted the majority of the sessions. Sitting down with grandparents or visiting the homes of well-known neighbors, these students gathered local stories, legends, anecdotes, recipes, and sayings. They were excellent interviewers. These young people knew their storytellers well and could often encourage them to tell a story they had told before. Those being interviewed felt more comfortable with the familiar interviewers than they would have with strangers, the usual collectors of folklore.

The conviction that young people should be involved in documenting the culture of their communities and that they can work as responsible researchers has been the basic belief of the Foxfire Project. Like that famous and most successful experiment, this three-year family folklore project conducted by the students of Tri-County High School has, I believe, made students more aware of a living history. This experience has given them a sense of a past different from that of the more formal story of history in social studies text books. It has shown them how we gather our attitudes of the past from the communities we grow up in, how we celebrate in recollection those selected events we choose to preserve, and how we weave fictions to explain the unsettling happenings. These students, working as field workers, have gathered a history "from below" which begins with what is most local and regional—the family.

Every family passes from one generation to the next stories which express a common past. This folklore binds a family together. *Plain Talk* is a collection of that folklore. It is also a collection of family photography from this region of Indiana. Students and members of the community brought us their old photographs so that we might copy them.*

This project has been made possible by an artist-in-residence grant from the Indiana Arts Commission through which I worked as writer-in-residence in the Tri-County School Corporation for three years.

Carol Burke

---

*The photographs do not reflect specific anecdotes within the book. Rather, they add visually to our understanding of the times and places discussed. —Editor

Coming Here

The story of a family's past often begins with the recollection of an ancestral journey: a migration to America, the passage to a promising region of the country, or the settlement in the town or village where the family now lives. In narrating their families' past our informants vividly retold what they had heard from parents and grandparents. Although these stories were part of the lore of particular families, we found shared characteristics: chance encounters, rendezvous that never took place, a naive central character (the traveler), hardships, and mishaps.

Although it does not recount a family journey, the narrative of Eva Talley is included in this section because it tells of her family's part in the Underground Railroad, that secret vehicle which conveyed blacks from slavery to freedom.

Coming to Indiana

Wilbert Cooper
talking to Tammy Cooper

When they came from Illinois they came by way of the railroad from Orlan Park in Illinois, and he landed here in Newton County in the middle of the night. They dumped him off where this elevator is over here at Percy. There was a Y, just a railroad Y they called it, where they turned around. They called it a Y because one branch went to Brook, see. But this was closer to where Dad wanted to go. He wanted to go just over the line — Jasper County and Newton County line — and just across the line. So he really moved into Jasper County.

Course, he was dropped out there in the middle of the night. He rode in the train with some cattle, a team of horses, and I guess maybe a little machinery. When he woke up in the morning and it got daylight, he thought maybe he could tell a little more about what he was doin'. He'd already been to the little grain station there at Percy where the regular road ran through. When it come morning then he had to guess. He didn't know one direction from another. But he looked around quite a little, and finally he figured, "Well, I'm goin' in the right direction." So he goes east which was proper, and he come to that place where Babcocks live now. There was a man there by the name of Sticknoth. He was a big fella, probably weighed 300 pounds and had whiskers all over his face. It wouldn't be uncommon today, but it was at that time to see a young man. But he was a big powerful man. And Dad knocked on the door and this big fella come to the door and pretty near scared him. A big stout fellow, but he was a nice friendly fella, and when he found out what Dad wanted to do, why, he say, "I'll go with you a ways and see that you get started."

Coming to America

Esther Bower
talking to Julie Bower

My grandmother, my mother's mother, came from — why, I don't know if it was Germany or I think it was in France she came from. Her brother had come over to the United States, and he liked it real well over there. And she was only sixteen years old so he wrote to her and wanted her to come to this country, so she came over. He told her he'd meet her. So she came to New York, and he wasn't there to meet her, and she never did find him. For several years she spent all she could make looking, advertising and looking for him and never did find him. And she was just a young girl sixteen years old and landed in New York and didn't know a soul. Never did find out whether he died before she got here or what happened. She never knew.

Finding His Sister

Esther Strasburger
talking to Tom Flora

My father didn't have any money, and he came to America to get away from the standing army in Germany. He had a sister here in America. And he was hungry, and he knocked on a lady's door and spoke German. She became very frightened and closed the door. So then he tried another door, and the lady said, "Well, I think you're speaking German, and I think there's a man that mends shoes who speaks German." She told him where to go. So he went to see this man who spoke German and was fed, and they got along beautifully. This man knew my father's sister in this country. That was surely a coincidence. And he got them together.

Contributed by Kenny Hughes

The Underground Railroad

Eva Talley
talking to Ellen Goad, Sally Waymire, Roger Emond, Tony Anderson, and Peggy Mormann

In our particular vicinity there were two stations. One on the hill west of us, and the other was my uncle's home about a half mile north from my home. And, of course, I was not born then, but my father was a little boy. And the same house stood there when I was a little girl. And they told me about what happened. And they had a room there, the front part of their house was a two-story house, and then in the back was a one-story which had the butchering room and the washing room, and all those chores were done out there. And it had a fireplace that backed up to the fireplace in the dining room of the two-story part of the house.

The slaves were being freed then, and they were trying to get from the south to the north. And they decided they would fix a place to hide the slaves. So between these fireplaces there was just a tiny space, and they made a sort of stairway up to the attic over this back part of the house. And this entrance to it was just a board just like the boards all along. It didn't look any different at all. So they would take that board out and take the slaves up into this place and hide them and then they would scrub very carefully the floors and everything where they might have touched. And when the masters came hunting for the slaves, why, they would ask if there were any slaves there, and they would invite them in and offer them a meal. They didn't exactly say that they hadn't seen them, but in a round about way left the impression they had no idea what they were looking for or what it was all about. And they would finally leave because they would go all over the house upstairs and down and into their cellar, and nobody was there. So they would go on, and as soon as they were safely away, my uncle would get the slaves down and quickly drive them on farther north to the next station. Or sometimes they would take them to the pond. In the spring there was always a big pond to the west of our house, and they would wade across the pond and stay on the other side. The dogs would get to the edge of the pond following the trail, and they couldn't find it any more. They would hide out there until they could take them on. So they helped many slaves to get away to the north.

Childhood

The major events in our lives are not the only memories we weave into stories about the past. Typically, recollections are colorfully threaded with ordinary happenings: the prank, the imagined world of childhood play, the unforgettable family vignette. These simple events shape the remembrance of childhood. Taken together, they give a sense of rural life, a life where the hired man played Santa, where the young child fell asleep on the corn wagon waiting for father to finish his work in the fields, where a birthday present might be bought for a penny.

Sleeping on the Corn Wagon

Norma Roberts
talking to Marshal Roberts

I used to go with my grandpa back to the fields. I won't forget that. We had a great big old long lane that led clear back to the back part of the farm, and we'd ride that old wagon. I would get up on that old wagon, and Grandpa with his team of horses would drive down the old lane. We would wait and wait and wait for Dad to shuck a load of corn. Back in those days it was shuck corn, not pick corn. I would wait for him too. I would get sleepy and fall asleep. So Grandpa, he'd just lay me back on the old load of corn (the ears of corn) and back up the old lane we'd come. He'd have to dump the corn, of course, and he'd leave me till the last second. Then he'd have to wake me up. I think I spent more time sleeping in the cornfield and on a corn wagon than I even did in my own bed in those days.

The Birthday Present

Catherine Behm
talking to Kathy Smith

I remember, too, when I was about six years old and my mother always baked big loaves of bread with yeast and flour, and all that. My mother's birthday came along, and I wanted to buy her a present. I didn't have any money, but I did have a penny, so I went to a store. I can see it yet. It was down in a basement of a building, and I bought my mother a cake of yeast which only cost a penny.

Contributed by Louise Ward

Christmas Tradition, I

Esther Strasburger
talking to Tom Flora

During the Depression we each had a plate on the table. When we got up in the morning there would be a banana, an orange, and some candy on each one's plate. That was our Christmas, but we were happy with it.

Christmas Tradition, II

Lillian Allie
talking to Cheryl McCollum

We'd hang our stockings on the door. They weren't little — they were rather big long stockings. We'd get up and have our dolls stuck down in our stockings, and in the top some candy my momma baked. But in the toe was almost always an orange. We had plenty to eat, whatever we needed, but once a year we would get an orange. I can remember that bright yellow. I couldn't bear to ever open them and peel and eat them 'cause they was so pretty!

Christmas Tradition, III

Catherine Behm
talking to Kathy Smith

Christmas was a big day for us kids. We were poor, and we didn't have enough money so mother couldn't give us a big Christmas celebration, but we were on a farm and my father had a hired man who took care of all the cattle. And we always looked for Santa Claus to come. And so the hired man would dress up like Santa Claus. He didn't look like the Santa Claus that we have today. He had old boots on and an old overcoat and an old cap hiding his face. And he came to our back door and threw oranges in our house and apples and candy. But when he came in with a box for each one of us — mine and my sisters' were always dolls. One of them had hair on it. The rest were glass headed dolls. My little brother would get balls and things like that. So the old Santa Claus used to come not on a sleigh but on a big white horse which Holland's people really believe in. They don't believe in a sleigh. It was always a white horse. We were really afraid of him, he looked so terrible with the big overcoat on and boots.

Contributed by Mrs. Marvin Nussbaum

Just Like Some Old Drunk!

Gwendolene Condon
talking to Kevin Palmer

I had an older brother, and you know what these older brothers are like when they're just about two or three years older than you are. I had a nice rag doll—I thought she was a peach. Well, my brother had a tub of water and a springin' board up above, and he told me it won't hurt my doll a bit. But do you know my doll, poor old Susie, had to lay around for two or three months to dry out. Just like some old drunk!

Playing Indians

Sam Gruber
talking to Susan Getz

In the spring of year out in Kansas it'd get so nice and warm, and the prairie grass would just begin to pick green up just a little bit. They had what they called Indian tobacco—we called it Indian tobacco. It looked a little like cotton. It would shoot forth out of the ground, and we'd chew that, and we'd say "That's Indian tobacco." It wasn't poisonous or anything, but we were playing Indians, see. And we'd put up our tents, and we would fix up a fireplace aside of a hill. We'd dig out a little hole, and we'd have our ventilation in the tent, and we'd have flat rocks to fry breasts of meadowlarks and sparrow breasts. In the summertime we'd get boiling water and have roasting ears there. Our meat would be breast of sparrows. Oh boy! You'd be surprised how much meat there was there, and same way with the meadowlarks. Then when the young rabbits would come along—they'd be about half grown. Oh boy! They were really good!

School

The country school, according to Nell English, had "heart." The place where children learned, socialized, and grew, the school, warmed by a pot-bellied stove, also offered a refuge to the transient looking for a night's shelter. Stories of school revive a place where teachers strictly imposed order and discipline that was continually challenged by the class rebels. Many of the stories about the schools of isolated, rural communities celebrate this defiance of authority. They tell of pranks which must have met with harsh punishment, but which, dimmed by time, are recalled with humor and a lingering admiration.

School Lunches

Lorean Wilder
talking to Roger Hensler

I went to a one-room school, and there was one and two in each class. There were eight grades, and usually the oldest would help with the smaller grades. In the wintertime we had a big pot-bellied stove, and we each took turns bringing potatoes or some kind of tomatoes to have soup. The oldest ones would make the soup. We'd set it on this old pot-bellied stove. It had a lid on top to cook the potatoes.

One would bring the milk from home, and it was whole milk then. And we had butter, and some of the mothers had made bread. Each one would bring for their day from home what they were going to have.

In the wintertime we'd walk to the Cucklebird Schoolhouse. When we got there (about a quarter of a mile), why, our feet would be froze or frosted so that the teacher would have to get some water, and we'd take our shoes and stockings off and put our feet in it till the frost started comin' out of our feet.

Learning to Spell

Gerald Forbes
talking to Ag Class

Well, Ruth Klink's father, that was John Humphreys, he taught school out there at the Black Oak School. (Several of the old people, they razz me about this now once in a while.) We were having spelling. Well, I was a little skeptical of whether I could spell the word *circle* or not so I wrote it exactly on the desk. I guess old John Humphreys, the teacher, must have saw me do it. He didn't miss a trick! And he came back there to my desk and wanted to know what that was there written on my desk. Well, I had to admit I'd written it down there, the word *circle*. I didn't think

14

I could spell it. I was gonna have a little trouble. Well, John hit me in the side of the head with one hand — *C*. Then he hit me with the other hand — *I*. Then *R*. And so forth till he got it done. Then he said, "Now do you think you can remember it?" He just about knocked me clear out of the seat each time! Well, Vic English was there, and he razzes me about that once in awhile.

Christmas Prank

Ruth Humphreys
talking to Eric Price

And then another prank that was quite popular when I first started to school in the country school was at Christmastime. The teacher expected it. They always did it, too. They would smoke him out. We just had a stove, a pot-bellied stove, in the middle of the school room, and, of course, you'd sit around there to try to keep warm. Well, the big boys would go up on top of the schoolhouse and put a board over that chimney and let that smoke all come

Contributed by Jerry Hensler

15

down, and smoke the teacher and the kids all out. So he'd say he'd treat us, and then they would go take the board off.

The Green Petticoat

Lela Martin
talking to Mark Lehe

The one thing that stands out in my memory about my early school days was one time when I was in the second grade. I think it was soon after school had taken up in the fall. My folks had made me what we called a petticoat in those days out of an old green jumper that was velvet (the bright green), and it came loose at my waist when we were marching around the gym. It fell off, and I was too embarrassed to do anything about it so the boys kicked it all around the room and finally kicked it into a corner. With a very red face I picked it up afterward.

Girls in the Outhouse

Hershel Deardurff
talking to John Deardurff

When I was goin' to school the girls—oh, about a dozen of 'em—would go to the outhouse and filled it up. I don't see how they ever got the door shut. Anyhow, we boys would go up there and shake it. We'd gradually shake one girl out at a time.

The Girl with Braids

Eva Talley
*talking to Ellen Goad, Sally
Waymire, Roger Emond, Tony
Anderson, and Peggy Mormann*

The first year that I taught school I had a boy in school who came from Indianapolis, and evidently they had a different system. He was used to having a play time about every fifteen minutes. So it just — He was an absolute nuisance, but he was there and we had to put up with him. So he sat behind a girl who had beautiful long hair. When it was braided it hung below her waist, and it was thick and brown and so pretty. But she insisted on putting the braids — When she would lean back against the back of her seat, she laid the braids across his desk. Well, I told her a time or two she better not do that because he didn't like it. But she did it. So one day when those braids were lying there, he took his knife out of his pocket and just cut those braids off right where they came over the edge of the desk. Well, she was just crushed, of course, and there was nothing to do. There were the braids and the short hair left on her head. So, of course, she felt like he ought to be punished — and I couldn't hardly keep from laughing. I thought if she had done what I told her to and not just tempted him and tempted him it wouldn't have happened. But she insisted that he ought to be punished, so I decided to give him a little whipping. And I took him out to the woodshed and took another boy along because I wanted to have a witness to it. So I whipped him. I don't think it hurt him very much. It sort of hurt his pride. But it eased her feelings. So that's one prank I always remember.

17

The Night Visitor

Nell English
talking to Bruce English

And talking about school businesses! I remember the time I didn't lock my door to the schoolhouse, and one morning I was coming to school. When I got within about a block of the schoolhouse a guy came out, and he left in a hurry. He had washed his socks and left them hanging on the stove. He got out of there before I did. He was watching, and he got out before I came in. He just wanted a place to stay all night. He had burned up most of the coal I had in. But back then the schoolhouse was warm because it had heart.

The Trustee's Visit

Lorraine Jones
talking to Ellen Goad

One time the trustee, who later became my husband, came to visit. And the children were always pretty good. I had a big room of them. I think there were forty-five. All at once they just acted so ornery, and I didn't know what was the matter with them. They'd giggle. And come to find out, he was sitting in the back of the room making faces at them. I was so mad at him I could have killed him!

The New Shoes

Jim Puett
talking to Brad Ulyat

I remember one time when I was a senior on the football team, why, the coach had to go to teacher's institute. He had to leave on Wednesday and come back on Saturday. We played on Saturday in those days. While he was gone the whole football team got together and went out and had a weenie roast. And of course when the coach came back, why, he found out about the weenie roast and being out that night, but he never suspected me (I guess I must have been a little angel). He never thought I was in with the gang and went.

I know I played harder that day than I ever played in any game in my life. I crawled off the field after it was over, I know. I felt bad, especially when the coach came — he brought me a new pair of shoes. Well, a new pair of shoes to a football player today don't mean anything, but we used to make our own football shoes. Put cleats on old shoes, and that's what we wore. And the coach brought me back new football shoes — I sure felt like a heel out of that deal!

The Loud Typewriter

Dorothea Wolfe
talking to Mark Molter

There were three young men who brought caps to school, you know for a cap gun, a toy pistol. They would hand them to me, and I would put them behind the typewriter keys and then start typing in class. The three young men and I were expelled from school for three days.

My mother was teaching, and I didn't see any peace. I thought I was going to lay in bed and enjoy myself, but I didn't. I got a sermon every morning and every evening.

BB's and Paper Wads

Irene Schmitz
talking to Tony Anderson

In high school we had some boys that played a lot of pranks on the teachers. They would get big handsful of BB's, and they would get clear back of the assembly room, give them a big toss, and they would go clear to the front of the assembly. At that time they had bookcases, and they'd hit the front of the bookcases, and the teacher in the front would look all around but she couldn't find the culprit. Also, they would make paper wads. They flipped them with their fingers clear across the assembly and tried to hit a teacher, or close to her. She'd look for the culprit, but she never could find him. But they didn't do too much 'cause our principal would slip in the back door when they weren't watching and would catch them.

Contributed by Louise Ward

Med School Prank

Richard Schantz
talking to John Erickson

Well, the only pranks that I would ever think that we did would be in med school, and that's because we had a girl in our class. There was only three to start with, and she was the only one who graduated. And we used to — She used to ride the streetcar, and we used to put different parts of the body in her coin purse so she'd have to get it out on the car. And we'd put fingers or ears or toes or something in there to make her get a little embarrassed when she'd get there.

Entertainment

Many of our contributors recalled with fondness the games they played as children, the organized sports they participated in as teenagers, and their courtship experiences. They made their own fun in the haymow, at basketball in the old blacksmith's shop, or at "town ball" when there were not enough for a baseball team.

Summer entertainment in this area of the state included the Fountain Park Chautauqua. Located a mile from the town of Remington, Fountain Park is one of the three surviving chautauquas in the country. Today, as it has for over seventy-five years, the chautauqua brings together several generations of families who for two weeks fill the small white cottages that encircle the shaded park (one of the few wooded areas in this fertile farm land). People come to renew acquaintances, to relax without television, to attend the religious services, to enroll in the painting classes, and to listen to music and visiting speakers.

─────────────────────────────

When We Got Caught

Gwendolene Condon
talking to Kevin Palmer

☀️

You know the Fishers lived across the street from us. Well, we called it an alley at that time, but it was as wide as a street. Our barns — The haymows faced each other, and our haymow window was higher than the Fisher one. Granddad wouldn't let us walk across that hay. He wouldn't even let us go up there to find a nest of newborn kittens. We had to wait till the momma kitten brought 'em down.

But anyway, there were enough of us kids between the Fishers and the Spencers and the Harts (the other druggist there in town) to have fun. We created ideas. We had — we found enough heavy wire and a pulley with a broomstick to it. And so we put the pulley through the heavy wire and stapled it to the head — to the top of each haymow window. Well, we slipped up the back way, and we'd hang on to the pulley and slide clear across that street, clear over to the Fisher barn. And then the big Fisher boys would lift us down, 'cause there were four or five feet that we'd have to drop.

Oh! We were having the time of our life. Now, I don't know who got the idea, whether it was Ma Spencer or Ma Fisher. But those two ladies, they were our mas you know. But they got out in the street. And they had those great long aprons. And you know how they'd put the aprons on their arms, hold one elbow with one hand and lean their head against the other hand? And they talked and looked, and they talked, and down they came and they said, "Kids! We'll give you just five minutes to get that thing down." Now, doesn't that sound like a couple of mas?

A Third of a Ghost

Marcella Kemp
talking to David Goy

We used to sit on a park bench at night, and there was a game we called "A Third of a Ghost." I don't know if that was the right name for it or not. It really wasn't ghost stories. You just started out with movie stars. You had to name a movie star whose last name began with *A*. Everybody took their turn, and finally when you run out of *A*'s and you couldn't think of anybody, then you start on the *B*'s and on down the line. And then if a person couldn't think of anyone three times he was out of the game.

Basketball in the Blacksmith's Shop

Anonymous
talking to Tammy Cooper

You wonder what we had for sports. We had an old blacksmith's shop that us school kids donated money to pay the rent on to play basketball in. This had a dirt floor in it, and we hauled sand in there so them cinders on the old floor wouldn't scuff up our knees when we played. We paid for all that ourselves. Sometimes the dust would get so thick in there you couldn't see your hand before you. That's how we got our sports furnished in our school years.

Town Ball

Charlie Murphy
talking to Kevin Clauss

Most of the ball we played in school was what we called "town ball," 'cause we didn't have enough to play baseball. We got them out by throwin' the ball between them and

Contributed by White County Historical Society

the base they was runnin' for. Now, you have somebody on every base, but we didn't have enough to go around for that. That's the way we played ball back then.

Date on a Bobsled

Ruth Humphreys
talking to Eric Price

I think I would've been a sophomore, a freshman or a sophomore. There was an awful snowstorm, and our school was closed. Out south of town here—where Martha Lemming lives—to that first corner on down there, the drifts were just even with the fence posts. You would have had to go through the field, and I couldn't go home because my folks would've had to come in the wagon. Well, they did come after me in the wagon after I'd been in town for about a week. But this one night we had a bobsled party, and a fella asked me if I'd like to go with him to Remington to a show, and that was really a big deal then. So we went in this bobsled—and oh, it was cold, but we had a good time. I was reminiscing with Mary Downing this week about it. I had forgotten all about it, and she said, "Yeah, I was along that night." And she said, "You remember, Ruth, about Ralph Miles tearing his pants."

I said, "Yes." We went to the show, and, I don't know, some way on the seat he ripped the whole front of his pants, and there it hung down. And you could see the bare skin. It was so cold, and like Mary said, we had all been wrapped up with safety pins and pinned up Ralph Miles' pants so he wouldn't freeze to death coming home. I think that was my first date.

Mishap at the Junior Prom

Ruth Humphreys
talking to Mark Lemming

I had a nice date when I was a junior, and I was going to the Junior Prom. It was in the old school building here at Wolcott. We had it in the hallway, and we decorated that hallway up and got some old Edison victrolas and had some settees in there to sit on. Everything was decorated with crepe paper. When you would come in the door from outside you would go up a little stairway and then would be in this hallway where we had this prom. It wasn't a prom. We didn't dance or anything in those days. It was just a little entertainment. We had taken crepe paper and made like a little hall down those big steps to make it a little more cozy looking.

When more people than we'd expected came to the Junior Reception (as we called it, not a prom because we didn't dance), we needed another tablecloth. The lunch was served in the first grade room. So they had to have another tablecloth 'cause there was more people there. Mrs. Lear, where I roomed and boarded, she sent me home to

Contributed by Ellen Goad

28

get another tablecloth. I went to run down those steps in a hurry and caught my heel and fell and grabbed ahold of that crepe paper and tore down all the decorations. I was pretty popular, I'll tell you, for a while! I had awful sore knees!

Fountain Park Chautauqua

Mabel Griffin
talking to Dave Milligan

The one at Remington I'm most familiar with. At one time I think there were hundreds of them established across the United States. These were the days before radio and television. The form of entertainment then was what everyone went to see. Now you can sit at home and watch it on television.

In those days the Chautauqua went for two weeks in the summer. It was started by churches. They would have their church services and also entertainment in the afternoon and evening. Also in the two weeks they would bring in what they called the Red Path Services who would have all kinds of entertainment — from music to singing to plays. All those things.

Now my father attended this and thought it was the most wonderful thing in the world. He would ride his bicycle. He and Ward Pampel would ride their bicycles into Remington — about five or six miles — and go to the Chautauqua and come home at night. You know it had to be very interesting. They dearly loved it. A lot of celebrities came. I know he has a picture of William Jennings Bryan, and I still have that. It was taken when he was there. Many people came that were famous in those days.

Today we only have, I think, three active chautauquas left in the whole U.S. One is at Remington, Indiana. The mother one, where it was started, was in Chautauqua, New York. There is one in Wisconsin, but I don't think it is as active as it used to be. I believe the Remington one is the only one that has never closed its doors to the public.

Chivaree, I

Bertha Grugel
talking to Shaun Schuh and Tina Black

They'd get a wheelbarrow and put that couple in and either take them around over town that way or maybe the bridegroom would have to wheel his bride around in a wheelbarrow. Then it got so they would take them in a truck and take them for a ride that way, and maybe wind up in some restaurant for their treat. Or maybe you had prepared something at home for your treat, but you always had a treat. You could either take them to a restaurant and buy something, or you could have something on hand at home to give them.

In later years they'd fit up that bed after the wedding with crackers or salt or sugar, pour that in. And of course, they'd like to do something with the folks' clothes if they possibly could get ahold of them. Maybe they'd sew the pajama legs shut.

Chivaree, II

Marilyn Carlson
talking to Brad Culp

If anyone got married we had a lot of fun. I can remember one in particular that I just loved. When one of my best friends were chivareed her husband had to wheel her down the main street of Crawfordsville in a wheelbarrow. While some of them were doing that, some of the rest of us went back to the house and took (I better not tell this) all the labels off their canned goods. When they went to open a can of something, they didn't know what they were opening for a long time afterwards.

Chivaree, III

Doris Faker
talking to Brent Faker

Oh, Dad and I had a good chivaree. Dad served cigars, and I served candy, and our friends came over from Reynolds. We moved here from Chalmers and Reynolds area. And I especially remember the next morning after the chivaree. We heard a funny noise and went upstairs, and there was a chicken. Some young man had gone out to the hen house and picked up a chicken and took it in the bedroom upstairs. That was the noise we heard. They came in, and we were just moving in. Everything was topsy turvy. But we had fun!

Halloween

Jean Best
talking to Karla Pangle

I will never in my life forget going to a party when I was in my teens. It was a Halloween night, and it was a rainy, stormy night. We hardly got in the door when they lined us up and turned the lights out, and they said, "Now we want to tell you about this accident that happen out here at the edge of town. And we went out to try to help pick up the pieces, the bodies that were so badly mangled." They proceeded to pass things to us to hold, and we had to pass them to our next neighbor. Some of the things were so gruesome that I have never forgotten that party. They had a rubber glove filled with cold wet sand and they said this was one of the hands. Well, in the dark and—A cold wet clammy fingers filled with sand certainly felt like a dead hand could feel. They had oysters, and they passed them and they said that these were eyes from the bodies. I can't recall too many other things, but those two things really frightened me. I just never forgot the party.

31

Upsetting the Outhouse

Jerry Cook
talking to Stan Cook

A guy named Sam Sigman lived in town, and every year the kids took upon themselves a real challenge to get Sam's outhouse because he got upset, irritated, and mad. He'd used a shotgun. I don't know if he ever fired at anybody, but he made everybody think he was going to anyhow. He'd fire in the air.

So three or four of us had parked down at Glen Oberlander's place and walked down to Sam Sigman's about two blocks away and upset his outhouse. Two crawled over the fence, and I was the one who didn't — I was chicken. But this one boy (and his dad used to be a teacher there in Wolcott), he jumped the fence and had on loafer shoes, the kind with no strings. As he got ready to leave real quick, why, one shoe flew off as he was climbing over the fence and Lowell Shoulz and me hauled him across.

Sam Sigman was outside on the back porch. He had his shotgun, and I can still hear him fire that baby in the air! We took off back to Oberlander's. That's where my car was at. I got back in the car, and these two boys got in with me, and we drove around for a little bit. We found out that Sam Sigman got in his car and was up town trying to find out what kids were in town. So while he was up there we drove down to their alley and let this boy out at one end of the alley. He ran through the alley and we picked him up at the other end. He had his shoe so we dropped him off at home, and I headed for home. That was enough!

New Technology

Comparing life in the present technological age with life fifty years ago, many of the people we interviewed described their fear and wonder at new inventions. To illustrate this naiveté they recounted their early impressions of the radio, airplane, and automobile — seeing, for example, the fence posts rush by at twenty miles per hour. As today, the autos of yesterday had chronic problems, but then, at least when a car would not start there was a team of horses to help. Not surprisingly, there is evidence that the special relationship between cars and adolescence was as strong then as now. For many of our speakers, their first car meant their first real independence.

The First Drive

Virginia Dodson
talking to Linda Furrer

I didn't own an automobile until I'd earned the money to pay for it. And when I taught over at Palestine I drove a horse, and Ralph Hamilton took care of it for me — they lived right across the road. And that year I bought a car, a Chevrolet coupe. I'd never driven a car before then, so I learned to drive. And I'd look out at the fence posts going twenty miles a hour, and it about scared me to pieces.

Early Automobiles

Glenn Meadors
talking to Dave Phillips

Back in those days you cranked them all. There were no self starters. You set the spark. One side had a lever on. It was the spark. The other was the gas. Then you went around and started cranking. Then you had a little wire on the front, and you pulled that wire to choke it. Then when she started, you ran around and got in, you see. In the wintertime they wouldn't start, and you had to pull them. Of course, you had to pull them with a team or one horse.

We had a team, and we put the harness on them and would pull this car down the road till she'd start. And when it started we'd unhitch'em and let them go back to the house and go to the barn. We'd go ahead and go to town. The team was so well trained that they'd just turn around and go back to the house. They'd go back and go in the barn, and when we'd come home from town, why, they'd be standin' there in the barn.

The Model T

Carl Thompson
talking to Brad Thomas

My first car was a Model T Ford. It was a coupe with rumble seats. It was a mighty nice automobile. I was working as a usher at the Colfax Theatre making three dollars a week. The car cost me a total of $125, and I'm proud to say that I had to pay for it entirely myself, supply it with gas, insurance, the whole bit, but I got the job done.

We was so stinking poor. I remember we would go swimming at the lake, and I had the car. The fellows who would ride with me would chip in a quarter for gasoline, and we would save fifteen cents so we could go over and buy a malted milk and take the girls home from the dairy parlor. That was all the kind of money we had, but we had a ball, just didn't miss money at all.

Banned from the Streets

Doris Faker
talking to Brent Faker

I can remember when we got our first sedan. That was a glassed-in car. And our neighbor called my mother and, "Oh," she said, "I'm glad we don't have a sedan. Just think if you'd have an accident, you'd just get cut." And you know, it wasn't very long before they had a sedan.

But I can tell you a good story about a car — this happened about 1909 — I had read it out of an old newspaper. A young boy got run over playing in the street. And this newspaper article said that cars should absolutely be banned from the city of Rensselaer, especially on a Saturday when children were playing in the street. Now isn't that bad?

35

First Airplane

Lydia McDonald
talking to Chris Annis

I can remember the first airplane I ever saw. I was scared out of my wits. We saw it in the sky, and we lay down on the ground. It passed. It was way up high and went on over. They didn't even know we were there.

That was when I was in Missouri and was a little girl. It was probably around the World War time.

First Radio

Mrs. Esta Nevins
talking to Melonie Bahler

We didn't have radio until we lived in St. Louis, and that was 1927. Our first radio was an Atwater-Kent, and it had a big speaker that stood up on top. I can remember when we first got that. We didn't have an antenna. We fastened the wires to the water pipes. The waterpipes in the houses went up on the outside of the houses. We stayed up till real late that first night, and we thought we had California and some of the states out west. I don't imagine we did, but we thought we did. We were getting quite a thrill out of it.

The Old Studebaker

William Misch
talking to Jeff Misch

The first car I owned was a 1931 Studebaker. It was a coupe that seated three people if you didn't mind being a little crowded. I paid fifty-five dollars for it. Bought it from my neighbor. We had an awful lot of fun in it. I was maybe about seventeen when I bought it, and we took a few—well, you kids today probably wouldn't consider them trips but back at that time, why, they were. We went to Michigan City to the beach in it and went to Lafayette, Rensselaer—And it was a pretty good old car. It had mechanical brakes, and the right front wheel (the brake on it) always grabbed.

I never will forget going up the main street of Michigan City one day. A lady and her little girl was standing there by the curb, and there was a stoplight there. Of course, it was green as we were coming up to it, and being young, we weren't slowing down too much. And just before we got there the light turned red. Naturally I slammed

Contributed by Terri Hensler

on the brakes, and the right front wheel grabbed and it locked the wheel. Of course the rubber burned and the tire squealed, and this poor lady grabbed the kid by the arm and about jerked her arm right out of the socket.

But we did have a lot of fun. We went to Winamac, and coming home one night we almost missed a curve and went around it on two wheels.

And it had one other bad feature. You never knew when you were out at night whether or not you'd have lights. Once in a while you'd turn the lights on, and they would come on. Once in a while you would turn the switch, and they wouldn't. I remember coming home from Wolcott one night on the back roads. I drove all the way to Rensselaer and got to the city limits in Rensselaer without any problems whatsoever, because everytime we met a car we pulled off the road and acted like we were necking. But there was just two boys in the car. We wasn't necking — we just had a way of looking like we were, so people didn't bother. So we made it clear to Rensselaer without any problems. We had just entered Rensselaer on the — well, let's see, it had to been southeast side (I happen to live on the northwest side), and as we came into Rensselaer we seen this one car coming at us. We pulled off the side of the road and stopped as we normally did, but it just happened that this car had seen us and happened to be the Rensselaer City Police. So they asked us what the problem was, and we told them the headlights weren't working. We couldn't get them to operate. But I said I had a sister and her husband who lived two or three blocks from there. So he said, "All right, you follow me down to their place, and you can borrow their car and go on home in it for the night." Well, they happen to have a Model A, and so I got them out of bed and got their keys and took their car. I started for home in it, and I had went about a half mile or so and the light went out on it! But he must of been patrolling another part of Rensselaer because I managed not being caught the second time, and we drove it for six months or so.

Work

In the lives of our Hoosiers, farms have grown from thirty to three thousand acres. Farmers whose days were once filled with the tending of livestock now perform chemical analysis on their soil, follow the commodities market, and take courses at Purdue University. The threshing (or thrashing, as is commonly said) crew which gathered at each farm for harvesting has been replaced by the lone farmer (or his wife) inside the air-conditioned cab of a big, green combine sweeping its way over the fields. Although the older farmers we talked with celebrated the technological advances of the last thirty years, they also nostalgically recalled a simpler time when there were no price supports and crop insurance, when the rural village, not the mall forty minutes away, was the social and shopping center for their families.

We heard stories, too, of life off the farm — stories of teachers, railroad workers, and small business owners, as well as the stories of enterprising young children. These stories of work hearken to times that were hard and to men and women strong enough to face them and to prosper.

My First Money

Eva Talley
*talking to Ellen Goad, Sally
Waymire, Roger Emond, Tony
Anderson, and Peggy Mormann*

I remember the first money that I ever made was for picking potato bugs off of the potato patch. My father told me he'd give me a penny a dozen for the bugs. If the first big ones were picked off there wouldn't be so many from the eggs laid, and they wouldn't have so many bugs. He used to use a Paris green. That's what we would use to finally kill them. But you had to pay money for Paris green so if you could cut down on the bugs you wouldn't have to use so much Paris green. So he told me he'd give me a penny a dozen. Well, I picked twenty-five dozen and got twenty-five pennies! And I went down to my uncle's store to spend my twenty-five cents. And he had some red calico with white figures in it, and I decided that would be nice for a dress. So I got enough of that for a dress which was five cents a yard. I was just a little girl, and three yards made a dress. That was fifteen cents. I had ten cents left! And I said, "What could I get for ten cents?" And he said, "Well, what about this little crock?" He had a little crock that would hold about—oh, over a pint—a little brown crock with a white edge. And that was just perfect, so I got a dress and a little brown crock, and I still have the little brown crock.

School Fireman

Sam Kilgus
talking to Steve Hofstetter

Had a pot-bellied stove. It was heated with coal, and I happened to be the fireman. I would go to school early, start the fire, and see that it was kept all day. I swept the school-

Contributed by Louise Ward

room out. When the rest of them came to school, I'd just about have my chores done, and I got ten cents a day.

Thrashing

Irene Schmitz
talking to Tony Anderson

Well, I used to go to Goodland, Indiana, to my cousins', two cousins—Dora Henderson and Goldie Henderson. They lived west of Goodland. I used to go up in the summer and help when it was time for thrashers. I would go up a lot before the men would cut the oats to make the shocks, or wheat, or whatever. And then when the thrashing run started—maybe about the last of July the first of August—the men that had the thrashing machine would come to the farm the night before with the thrashing machine and separator. They would park them where they were going to do their thrashing. They'd get their belts and everything on the machinery and everything all set up so the next morning they could get up early and start up the firing of the big engine, the steam engine. They always had a load of coal with them.

They'd start up their engine and get the steam built up in the big boiler, and they always parked where they could get water, because you always had to have your boiler full of water. Well, a lot of times, if a horse tank was close by and it was clean, they would siphon that off very carefully and use that in the boiler. But sometimes they would have to go maybe miles to a creek where they could get clean, more clear water to fill the boiler. Then they would use the steam for the power for their big thrashing machines.

We used to take—My cousin would take gallon jugs, the old fashion pottery-like jugs, white pottery. They were enclosed in burlap, then inside between the jug and the burlap they stuffed straw, so it was sort of like an insulation around the jug. Then she would take a gallon of real cold water and maybe put a tablespoon of lemon. She squeezed lemons and took a tablespoon of lemon juice and poured it in that and shook it. She said that that will keep the men from getting overheated if they had the lemon, the juice, the acid. I suppose vinegar would do the same thing. So we would take those jugs, carry them out to the field where the men were working so they all had plenty of water when it was so hot.

The Thrashing Ring

Hugh Jackson
talking to Denise Dotson

I remember when I was just a kid, and they had a thrashin' ring. I wasn't hardly big enough to do much then, maybe throw a few bundles on, but I just loved to be out there. They was thrashin', when I was a little shaver, with steam engines, and I remember well the guy that run the steam engine. There was two boys, the Keltch boys, that run the outfit — Henry and Charlie. Henry run the separator, and Charlie run the engine. Charlie was just a little puny-like fella, little wiry guy, and he always liked to come to Sam Jackson's place (that's my father's name). We always had some good, short copper rails for him to use. That was short rails I speak of, rails that one end had probably rotted off and we couldn't use 'em. We had a kinda little short-handled ax there, and I never saw anybody handle an ax as good as what he did. But boy he really liked to burn them copper rails, and we usually run eight bundle wagons. That thrashin' machine there was pretty good size. I don't know how big the cylinder was, but I know anyhow it run eight bundle wagons.

And at that time, all grain was sacked in that country from the thrashin' machine. There was a lot of local flour mills there where they made flour. What went to the mill, they was put in two bushel sacks. They was a kind of a canvas sack, and of course we could load them on the wagon. Usually, oh, about a hundred bushel of them — Had to be about fifty sacks. That country is a little bit rolling, and of course it made a pretty good load for some of our teams. But like I say, there wasn't any dumps there for the

43

wagons—it was all in sacks then. They had to hand that out, and then it went back in, and it was dumped inside the mill. And mostly wheat in that country. They raised a little bit of oats, but not very much, mostly wheat and some rye. And you talk about the wheat yields! Now they run fifty bushel! Sometimes sixty! At that time if we got twenty it was a pretty good wheat yield. And thrashin' was a big event. I don't know, I suppose it probably took in about twelve families or so.

Age limit for working hadn't come in much at that time, especially on the farm. But most of 'em was, oh, about high school age before they'd be runnin' the bundle wagon or carryin' grain or pitchin' or anything like that. The youngest one that was on there was the water boy, when they had the steam rig especially. He's the one that took the water around to the field. He took a jug of water, just a plain old stone jug with a sack wrapped around it. The sack had been soaked in the horse tank or something there so the outside of it would keep cool. After all, a sack that's evaporating will keep cool. Another guy, a rather young-like fella, was the guy who run the water wagon. He had to haul water from a local stream or a pond for that steam engine. And, uh, that was pumped by hand. They had a hand pump with a long handle on it, and they dropped the hose in and pumped that out of someplace—a creek, small creek, or else a pond—and hauled that there.

Contributed by Louise Ward

44

And the thrashin' dinners, well, they consisted of about everything but the dishrag! You just name it, and we usually had it: fried chicken (that was very common for that was about the time the chickens would be along in season), whatever meat they had, three or four different vegetables, jelly-'n'-jams and preserves was very common in that country, pie, and cake. But don't forget one thing now, we didn't have any refrigeration at that time, and they didn't really need very much for there wasn't much left anyhow. By the time you run about two tables of men through that pretty well took care of things. I did work in one thrashin' ring after I was outa high school there, where we thrashed up till dark, and then we had supper. We didn't stop for supper, and we'd just eat supper in shifts.

Now you talk about a forty-hour week! There wasn't any forty-hour week. I took the lantern to the barn with me in the morning to harness the team, and when I got back the kid was out there with the lantern for me to put the team up in the evening. You can figure yourself how long a day it was!

Hire a Man with Patches

Ed Kyburz
talking to Sandy Kyburz

My dad always told me whenever he hired a man, a farmer, he would hire somebody with patches on the front of his pants, but he wouldn't hire a man with patches on the back of his pants. He said he got the patches on the front from working, and he got the patches on the back from sitting down all the time!

Wages

Henry Provo
talking to Brad Culp, Brent Faker,
Lee Farney, Scott Bahler, and Jim
Burrell

Corn got down to about eight cents I think. So did the hogs get down to pretty near nothing. I remember going to town with Dad one day taking a load of corn, and we brought back just a little bit of coal to burn.

And after I was old enough to where I was working out, we'd shuck corn for a cent a bushel. You had to shuck a hundred bushel a day to make a dollar.

The Work of a Dairy Farmer

Anonymous
talking to Betty Miller

If you go back, thinking back into those times, a lot of things was done with horses. With a horse, it's a little different than the tractor. You don't just turn them off. And you don't just turn them on the next day. The horse had to be fed three times a day. Usually they would have some kind of grain. Oats was real popular, and a little bit of corn. Feeding a horse — You can't feed them too much corn because they will get too fat. They don't work well. They work better by feeding a blend of shell corn. And you didn't run into town and get a couple hundred pounds of shell corn. We shelled it by hand with a hand sheller. Now that's not — I don't mean shelling by hand where you broke grain off with your hand. On the farm there they had what we called a hand sheller. And this was on a wooden box that was about, oh, twenty-four inches wide and about thirty inches long and about twelve to eighteen inches deep. And you would shell this full. Take your eared corn and shell off this box of corn and keep corn ahead. Then you would sack it up. Maybe you would shell a couple shellers full or whatever it's going to take to feed the amount of horses you had. Also, you would feed this shell corn to your cattle, too.

I might go a little farther on about those chores a little bit here. Almost every farm had milk cows, because in those days you didn't buy your milk — you had enough cows to have your own milk supply. Plus you would sell your milk if you had more milk cows than you could use the milk from. It was all done by hand. As an example, as I recall on our home, there we had about eight milk cows. Now, you might have one or two that would be, shall we say, dry. They wouldn't be milking. They would be having calves later on. And with these calves, you would raise them and some of them you would butcher for your meat.

But going back to the milking a little bit — They used a small bucket to usually milk in so that you could handle it. It would be like a twelve to fourteen quart-size bucket. You would have to carry these buckets from the cow barn where you were milking up to wherever you handle your milk. And you would, say, milk — As an example, we usually had about four milk buckets, and we would milk these full. And then we would take them up to where we handled our milk. You carried it up to the place where you store your milk. And often, most all the time, this was outside. You would have a tank there. In the winter time, you might have to set the cans inside so they wouldn't freeze. And the way the milk was handled, you had a strainer, and this strainer had a cotton type pad in it. You would pour the milk into this strainer. It would hold a couple gallons at a time. The milk would run through the strainer into the cans. Milk cans were similar to what you see in the antique stores or about ten gallon size. And this milk, then as I said, if it was cold it had to be stored inside so it wouldn't freeze into the cans. Then it would be set out on the mornings for the man that came to pick up the milk. And they would usually come about every other day. So that meant that you had to handle the milk and keep it from freezing if it was cold weather. If it was warm weather, you could take the containers into a trough or tank and put water around them to keep them cool. So this would keep them a lot cooler. You had to keep changing this water every day.

47

So that meant every day it was hot you had to change the water. The milk people that picked up the milk started early in the morning so they could try to get their route picked up before the heat of the day. If you were milking and you had some, if you were on the first place on the route, you would have to get up early in the morning and have your milking done. As an example, the man might come pick up the milk at six in the morning. That meant you had to have your cows in. You had to have them fed. You had to have them milked. You had to have the milk up at the tanks where it is going to be picked up, in the cans, ready for them at six. If you had to be up and have this done by six, this meant you might have to get up at four-thirty or five to do it. So if you try to get up at four-thirty or five in the morning, you soon find that you can go to bed at eight in the evening.

Contributed by Louise Ward

First Teaching Job

Avanelle Brooks
talking to Brent Stanley

When I started teaching it was, oh, right after the First World War, and I wanted to teach up near Huntington where I had a favorite aunt. I wanted to be close there so I had written, and they had told me that they had a place for me in a consolidated school where I would have three grades. My father took me up there, and they told me that the teacher who had taught it before hadn't intended teaching that year, but her husband was just home from service, and he couldn't find a job (in those days they didn't give the soldiers their jobs back, they didn't reenlist), so she wanted her job back. So all that was left was a country school, and I decided, well, it was the only thing to do.

I had gone to school, and I needed the job so I took it. But there was one hitch, they told me that the teacher who had taught it before had had to leave, that the kids ran her out. I was a little skeptical about it, but they said they'd had to have a man finish the year of school. But I went in there. I was only seventeen years old, but I went in there thinking they might run me out, and I was amazed when I saw those kids the next day. They were the sweetest kids you could imagine, and I didn't see how they could ever do anything. They didn't to me. They were just wonderful.

As I told you I was just seventeen years old, and I had a little girl in the fourth grade who was sixteen years old, and she should of been in an institution of some sort. Her mother had died, and she lived with her father and several brothers. One day there was a rap at the door, and the sheriff and the welfare lady came. I guess they didn't call them welfare in those days, but they came and they took this girl away with them. Well, I hadn't talked to the parents or anything. I didn't know what was what, but they said it was all right. And they were going to put her in the Fort Wayne school for a while. I can't think of the name of the school, but they had to keep her in the jail until they could find a place in a home for the feeble minded. And so we felt bad that she had been taken away.

But the next morning I started out for school (and I lived about a quarter of a mile away) and I was walking, started out with my lunch box. I got out to the corner of the house, and there came a man up over the hill with a gun over his shoulder, and of course I was frightened. I ran back into the house and had the landlady look and she said, "Oh yes, that's her father." So she called all along the road to town and they, everybody, traced him until he came. And then we found out he had taken his gun to the hardware store to sell it. But all day long everybody was so afraid that that man was going to come out and shoot us all up.

That first year I made sixty-five dollars for seven and a half months of school.

The Sixteen-Hour Law

Jim Puett
talking to Brad Ulyat

My dad was an engineer for the old Vandalia Railroad in Logansport, and I remember when I was a kid when my dad would be gone for two weeks at a time and I'd never see him. That was before laws like the Sixteen-Hour Law took effect, a law that said an employee could only work sixteen hours. He couldn't work any more. After that law was passed he'd get on the road, and after sixteen hours he'd stop the engine and wait till somebody else come on to take his place. And then he would have to have eight hours before he could be called out again. So then I used to get to see him once in awhile. But there was times before the Sixteen-Hour Law went into effect that my dad would be gone two weeks and only maybe be in for four hours. He'd be in when I was asleep and leave when I was asleep. So I watched the development of what they called the Sixteen-Hour Law in railroading.

The First Beauty Operator

Lillian Allie
talking to Cheryl McCollum

I'd like to share a little story about our first beauty operator here in Wolcott, which would have been in about 1930 or something like that. There wasn't any beauty parlor or beauty operator here when we moved here in town. My Edith (who is married to David Dellinger now — she's Mrs. David Dellinger), her and her sister had learned to use wave set and make pin curls. There wasn't anyone else here, and so they did it in my home. They just had, oh, just had all they could handle to do just with wave set and bobby pins. And they got thirty-five cents apiece — that's what they got for what they did.

Playing for the Symphony

Robert Winger
talking to Scott Winger

We took lessons from an old Chicago man that was the greatest solo there, for nine years. He was pretty tough, and so when we got through the nine years he said, "Now I've taught you about all I can teach you, so now you have to get out in public." We didn't have nowhere to go so we went to Lafayette. I remember the first time I went down there. We went up above Niswonger's Jewelry Store for the first time. We got up there to take interviews for the Concert, four of us, walked in there and, boy, you kinda felt funny. There were about thirty-five men sitting there. You never seen one before. Never seen the director. But he lifted his baton and give us the swing, and off we went. We never had no problem. We played that interview there, and he come down and he said, "You've got a job for the summer." So they started a symphony there, and we went into that and played awhile and played around different places with some of the leading band men, and we got along just fine. We liked it. Then the kids got married and got gone and kinda give it up. But I still love music. I like good music, and that's all I played.

Snake in the Spinach

George Scott
talking to Peggy Mormann

Well, I was a very good, nice young gentleman; however, on one occasion, temptation got the better part of me. I do recall that as a fifteen-year-old kid I was working in the field with Mexicans. And on this particular occasion, we were cutting spinach for the cannery where my dad was superintendent. And one of the Mexicans killed a snake, and myself and my companions (a couple other kids from town) thought it would be a nice trick if someone stuck that in a hamper of spinach and sent it to the factory. So I promptly dumped it into the hamper, covered it up with a little spinach. And now you have to understand what happened when the spinach gets to the factory. There are two men whose job it is to dump the hampers on a large belt, conveyor type belt, which runs past two rows of ladies sitting there sorting the weeds, mud, and things like this out of the spinach. Well, these fellows dumped the hamper out. The spinach came down the belt with the snake and all you-know-what broke loose on the sorting line. My dad tried in vain for quite some time to find out who did that, and he was going to fire whoever that was. Of course, I didn't know who did it. That was about the worse thing I ever did. There were a lot of other things I guess, but they weren't that much.

I Learned a Lesson

Anonymous
talking to Marcia Furrer

One time we were going to Cleveland with a load of pota-toes, and I took the truck this particular trip. When we got in there to the dock to unload, why, I noticed we couldn't unload our trucks like we did before the war. The union had come in, so we had to hire a couple of guys to unload our truck. I noticed that these guys, when I paid them, they kind of looked over my shoulder and seen how much money I had in my billfold. I never gave it a thought, I fig-ured that the war was over and we were back in the States where it was safe. But then when I left, they asked me what route I took out of the city. As I left then I pulled up to a stop sign and here some guy jumps on my running board, and I didn't have the doors locked, and he crawled right on in and put a gun in my ribs. He told me to turn at the next corner. Well, I did as he said. He said he had some friends that wanted me to haul some stuff back to Indiana. I said, well, boy, that sounds good because we like to haul both ways with the truck because it pays off better. I knew that I would have to kind of go along with him. So after going about four blocks he had me pull up in front of an old car garage, and there was a couple of guys that pulled a cur-tain back and was looking out. I was looking for extra guys because I figured he wasn't alone, and sure enough I spot-ted these two guys that unloaded me. So as we pulled up in front of the garage I acted like I was going to get out of the truck. I just opened my door; and while I was doing it I slipped it down in low, and as soon as I seen he had his door open I gave him a big shove and I took off. I just looked back once and seen him crawling up, and the two guys came out and picked him up and carried him in the garage. So that taught me a lesson after this: if you go into a city you keep your doors locked.

Hard Times

Hard times — the crisis an individual has survived, family setbacks, collective hardship — are the core of memory. The stories of these times define a people and the values of a community. They display the resilient self-sufficiency of a people "making do" with next to nothing and celebrate in retrospect a period of scarcity as a time of challenge met and overcome. No one doubts that the individual is strengthened, the family more tightly knit, and the community solidified by trial.

Underlying all these statements is an ultimate trust in the land. For many of these speakers the land is all you can trust. Husbanded properly it will provide. To lose one's land is the only true catastrophe; to take someone's land, true villainy. The passage of years has not dissipated the anger felt for the bankers' agents who, during the Depression, foreclosed on mortgages and those who took advantage of impoverished farmers by purchasing their defaulted mortgages at twenty dollars an acre. Countless are the stories of dogged thrift adopted as the only means of reversing disaster. By putting aside a little of next to nothing every week, families could hope to buy back the farm and to own again the only place where they could belong.

First Job

Ruth Humphreys
talking to John Lemming

My mother died with tuberculosis when I was nine years old, and we lived out in the country. I was very lonely that summer.

There was a tomato canning factory nearby us called Ox Valley. My brother worked there, so I could go with him, but we had to walk. That's the only way we had to go, and it was a couple of miles over there. I'd walk there every morning and home in the evening, and we'd take our lunch. Then I was too young to be allowed to really work there, but another lady, when the inspector would come around, would pretend that I was her little girl. I would stand by her, and I would put my tomatoes that I peeled in my own bucket so that I would get, oh, about a cent or something like that a bucketful of tomatoes. I worked all summer I think and made thirty-five cents.

Foot Stones

Sue Sutton
talking to Rhonda Sutton

I can remember at that time we didn't have a furnace, and our upstairs wasn't heated, so my mom would heat foot stones and wrap them in towels and put them in the foot of our bed to warm our bed up.

They're about a nine by six stone. They're about an inch thick, and they had holes in each side of it. You would put it in the oven and get it hot, and you'd take a wire and stick it in those holes and take it out, and wrap it in a blanket or a towel, and take it and put it in the foot of your bed.

I Tried to Carry On

Esther Strasburger
talking to Tom Flora

We lost our mother in 1922. I was just a young girl, and I was the oldest one at home. My father died two years later, so we were just a bunch of orphans. There were eight of us, and I was the oldest one. There was one other boy that was out of school that did the farming. I wanted the twins to go on to high school. And he said, "If they go to high school, I'm quitting," so they didn't get to high school.

I tried to carry on like I'd seen my mother do so many years—make bread, why, I had to make bread. And the first batch I ever made, we couldn't even eat it. I laid it out there by the washhouse, and the chickens picked at it and picked at it. Then when it rained, they finally ate it. But I really learned to make bread after that. Practice, I guess, sure helps. And then I always made a hundred buns every time I baked bread, which was about three times a week. And the last thing before I went to bed I worked those buns out, and then you bake them the first thing in the morning. Well, you can imagine eight of us, we could all eat three apiece and then send three apiece in their school lunches. The buns didn't last very long. So I guess I really learned how to make them. We really ate them!

The Depression was really rough on us because we went through the Depression without our parents. If my dad didn't own the farm I don't know how we would have managed. I made all the girls' clothes and made the little boys' underwear, the big boys' BVDs. I did a lot of sewing for the kids, and many times I sewed till twelve o'clock at night so that they would have clothes to wear. The two younger girls were very, very good to help me, or I never could have done all I did without them.

He Wore His Sister's Coat

Ruth Humphreys
talking to John Lemming

Well, we had 280 acres that was in the farm. And we had a team of mules and a couple of old Jersey cows and two or three brood sows and about fifty hens, and that was it. We thought we was as well off as anybody. Nobody had much in those days, and if you had one outfit for Sunday you were pleased. And John wore his sister's coat to church on Sundays because we were too darned poor to buy him a coat. And Martha's coat was still good, and I was too stupid to know to take the chinchilla off of the tail of it and around the collar, so he wore it like that till Mary Downing felt sorry for me and give me one of Charles's old ones.

The Barber

Mac Dismore
talking to Carol Burke

Way back when I was a kid here in Wolcott I started shining shoes, and we had what we called the bath concession. Now this goes way back. When I was a kid, I suppose nine or ten years old or even younger, I would sweep the floor, and we had a bath tub. Now we had a little room, and it cost you a quarter to get a bath. What we furnished there was a clean towel and soap. I would of course scrub out the tub between each bath. I'd spread fresh newspaper on the floor and then my dad, he in turn would furnish the hot water, and I'd give my mother fifty cents a week to wash the towels. And on a Saturday, between shining shoes and the bath concession, I'd make five and six dollars, which was a tremendous amount of money.

Back in those days the businessmen got shaved every morning. The barber shops at one time opened at six o'clock and closed at ten, eleven o'clock at night. But it was quite cheap for you to get shaved. You didn't shave yourself—that was before the days of safety razors and electric razors. And everybody just had to line up there every morning to get their morning shaves.

One day my dad didn't like the way the banker was talking when he came for his shave. He came home and told my mother, he says, "I don't like what he's saying." So Dad took his money out of the bank. For about two years we had between $700 and $1,000 under our dining room rug. In the meantime, everyone went broke, and Dad would loan the money out to buy teams of horses and things like that, and at a little interest, of course. But I didn't get my money out, though. I took it out of the first bank and went over and put it into the other bank. Then Roosevelt declared the bank moratorium, and the bank I was in then never recovered, so I lost it.

We survived. Back in the Depression my dad had the barber shop, and we saw a lot of people more unfortunate than us come in there. An individual would come in, and he'd say, "Is there anything I could do to wash up and clean up a little bit?" He probably had on a frayed white shirt, but you could tell that until he was laid off he had held some sort of an executive position. You could distinguish those from the fellows that would come in and say, "Ah, how about a nickle for a hamburger?" or "How about a nickle for a cup of coffee?" These other fellows would say, "Could I wash the windows? Can I wash the floor? Is there anything I could do?" There for a couple of years my dad always had a place where they could get hot water or they could shave.

During that time was when I learned to barber. We had families that had two, three, four or five kids—boys, I'll put it that way. As I say, it was quite popular then to keep your hair short. I learned on the kids. The dad could afford to pay the thirty-five cents for his hair cut, but he couldn't afford to pay for four haircuts. So I'd cut their hair, and my dad would step over and say, "Take a little more off here, Mac," or "Take a little more off there." I still have some personal friends that live around here, and they say, "I can remember when you used to cut our hair and whittle away on me when we didn't have the money."

It was quite an experience, that Depression. People

would come in and trade suits and trousers and what have you. And they would pick up newspapers. At that time we had a tile mill here in town, and they would take those newspapers, spread them out, and sleep under them at night.

The Price of Things

Ceil Schafer
talking to Beverly Kenoyer

Well, it was rough. We didn't have very much money, and we didn't get much money for what we sold. Corn was fifteen cents a bushel, and the yield was twenty-five bushel per acre. The oats was nine cents a bushel, and the yield was twenty-five or thirty bushel. Eggs were six cents a dozen, and cream was fifteen cents a pound. Hogs was two cents a pound. Land price at that time was sixteen dollars an acre to thirty dollars an acre. My aunt and uncle, they bought 120 acres for $3,600. Wages for a man who worked on a farm was eighteen dollars a month. Once in a while they might get twenty dollars. We managed on cream and egg money. When we went to town we would get, why, maybe like a quarter's worth of sugar, a quarter's worth of rice, a quarter's worth of navy beans, and we liked fig bar cookies and ginger snap cookies, and we'd get a quarter's worth of those. You got a nice sack full when you bought for a quarter like that.

Mortgage payments was just almost impossible for people to pay. The Federal Land Bank was real good, and they would cut the principal off and the people would pay the interest. The interest rates on a loan at that time was three and a half percent. I can remember, also, my aunt and uncle (they had nine children in their family), and he had no work, and my aunt was sick. I would walk over to their house, and that was two miles. I'd carry baskets of food for them. Each day I'd go over there. Then the neighbors would give them separated milk. And things was really rough.

The Depression

Hershel Deardurff
talking to John Deardurff

The Depression was like hell; half enough to eat and no money to spend.

Burning Corn

Ray Smith
talking to Rob Fulkerson

One year there in the early thirties, we were thrashing in the summer on our oats crop, and the oats were eleven cents a bushel. It made it pretty hard for the tenant to pay the thrashing bill and try to make ends meet with all the expenses. As it went along into the fall of the year, corn husking time (it was shucked by hand, and corn was down to nine cents a bushel), but as it went along through the

Contributed by Louise Ward

winter, why, corn began to work up a little and that next summer it got up to twenty-five cents a bushel. But all fall and winter a lot of people burned corn. Any spoiled ears or anything, they just threw it out to the side and burned it. They didn't bother about feeding it, it was cheaper than coal, and it made good fuel. There was lots of corn burned that winter for fuel because people didn't have the money to buy coal, and corn wouldn't buy the coal.

The hog prices were around two-fifty to three dollars a hundred, and it just made it pretty near impossible to pay the bills.

The Price of Gasoline

Bertha Grugel
talking to Shaun Schuh and Tina Black

It was pretty tough going. There was lots of times we were selling gas, and we had one customer that every time he came to town he'd buy fifty cents worth of gas. And we had understood that he went home and put some kerosene with it in order to make enough mileage to get back again. He lived about ten miles from Wolcott.

The Family Land

Robert Winger
talking to Scott Winger

My father pretty near had his farm paid for, then he lost it in the Depression. The Depression really hit everyone, and it didn't any of them escape. I can remember they was going to take a farm from a family north of town (I won't mention the name), and I got a call one morning and they said, "We want you to come to Monticello."

I said, "What do you want me to do in Monticello?"

They wanted me to go see a loan company. They was going to foreclose on this land. So we went up there, and

62

there was about seventy-five people in the courthouse, and they wanted to get hold of this loan man. They was really going to work him over to not foreclose, but the sheriff came down and says they got him locked up and nobody can see him. So one of them got a rope, fixed it up with a hanging noose on it, put it in there. They had quite a time, but we went out, and they didn't foreclose on this man. And they still own the farm today.

I bought the homeplace that my father lost in the Depression. I always wanted that, so one day I was in town, I saw two men drive through in a car, and they told me they was real estate men. I stopped them in town and told them I wanted to buy a farm, and they said, "Do you have any money?"

I said, "I don't have a dime."

"Well, how do you expect to buy a farm?"

"Well," I said, "I got some stock, and I got some furniture and one thing or another."

"Well," this one guy says, "We'll see what we can do."

So we went to Chicago in February. It was cold, man it was cold. Went up in the Pure Milk. There was a lot of offices up there, and we'd never been there before so we got ahold of the manager. He wanted to know what I wanted, and I told him.

He said, "Why, you ain't got any money."

I says, "That's why I come here for it." And I says, "I want to borrow some money."

"Well," he says, "it's really not our business."

I says, "But I sell my milk here, and you know about it."

And he says, "You go on home, and we'll talk it over and let you know in a few days."

So the fellow I went up there with and I, we kinda decided that was all. But in a few days we got a letter, and he said I could have the money. So I bought this farm my father lost, and with seven boys kept them busy. I didn't let them loaf, and we accumulated that. Of course, it didn't cost very much. I think we gave around seventy-five dollars an acre, and at that time nobody wanted the land anymore at one and a half percent interest.

So we got it paid off, and the boys kept gettin' married, and they wanted to get into business, so we just kept buying a little more (not any more than we could pay for) as we went along. Give each one a home, and we got one in the fertilizer business. They all got their homes, and we're thankful for them. The Lord's been good to us. We got nice grandchildren, and we just hope and pray that they will be saved some day and be able to spend Eternity with us in a New Heaven and a New Earth.

Putting Away a Ten or a Twenty

Gerald Forbes
talking to Matt Lile

We had a bit of a farm that had came down from my mother, and my dad had the use of it as long as he lived. Well then my sister and I would be left, and I didn't think that she was going to be in the position to buy it. And I thought, well, I'd better start thinking about it. So the old bank building in Wolcott had a bunch of lockboxes, and I had one of those rented to keep my papers that I didn't want to lose in. And I had the idea that whenever I could pull out my purse and take twenty dollars or ten dollars out of my purse and get along without it, then I would drop it in my lockbox. And I persistently kept putting some in there. I thought to myself, "Now, I'm not going to count it." I never went back and counted it. Now days, this would be foolish, with interest and so forth. There wasn't any interest then, but I persistently kept putting a ten or a twenty in that box.

Shortly before my father died I had bargained to buy 110 acres of pasture land just west of me. When my father died, of course, my sister wanted to settle up right away. She said, "I can't buy it. You'll have to buy it." All at once I thought, "I gotta have some money." I went to this lockbox, and believe it or not, (of course, land wasn't that high then) I paid for that 110 acres of pasture out of that lockbox, paid my sister off, and I had a thousand and I think about 600 dollars left over. Now that is by persistently putting a little aside. And I never missed a dollar of that that I put in there. I got along without it.

A Letter to the President

Lula Fisher Ulyat
talking to Kim Holder

Well, the Depression was so bad that my first husband and I got behind two payments on our home — the home I live in now. We had been all over the country trying to borrow money, and we couldn't get it anywhere. So finally, unbeknownst to my husband, I wrote a letter to the President of the United States. It was President Roosevelt. And I hadn't anymore than got the letter in the post office only a couple of days till here comes the guy that sold us the house. He wanted to show it; he had a man with him, and he wanted to show him all over the house. I said, "Why do you want to do that?" He said, "Because you're back two payments, and we want to sell the house." I said, "Well, you're not going to do anything of the kind because I've written to the President of the United States for help, and I'm sure we'll get it!" I reached up and locked the screen door so they couldn't come in. He left, and I think was swearing under his breath as he left the house.

At the very end of that same week I got my letter from the Secretary of State, signed by the President. They referred us to the Home Owners Loan Company at South Bend, Indiana. They said all we had to do was just write them a letter that they had written, and they were going to help us. So that's how we finally got the house paid for.

We Could Live Off the Land

Irene Schmitz
talking to Tony Anderson

It was mostly in September and October in 1929. Things began to get pretty tough. We were living in Watseka, Illinois. My husband had a real good business, but a firm in Grand Rapids, Michigan, wanted him to come up there and become the foreman and part of the furniture factory. That was the Sly Brothers which manufactured high class bedroom furniture. We sold everything we had but his tools and a few items we wanted to keep and moved to Grand Rapids, Michigan, in October 1929.

Things were real good for about two months. Then bang, buildings became empty, businesses closed, firms went out of business, things became scarce. Work was scarce, and people had no money. So a good many people bartered or traded what they had for something somebody else had, maybe wouldn't use. So that way a lot of people got along. That was the barter system, and it lasted for about four or five years.

But we moved from Michigan back to Brook, Indiana, in the next winter after the Depression started. We lived in Brook until the next spring then moved out on a farm. We had a cow, a pig, chickens, and we had a big garden. I sold eggs. I sold dressed chickens, made cottage cheese. I sold butter. I sold vegetables, and we got along real well because we could live off the land.

We Were Just Poor

Ruth Humphreys
talking to John Lemming

We were just poor like everybody else. We made our own amusement. We'd go down to the neighbors and maybe make a little preserve ice cream, or a plate of taffy, or something to amuse ourselves with.

And it came Christmas time this one year. We had three children: Martha, John, and Jim, and they were all three small. And so we didn't have any money to really buy Christmas presents with, but our neighbors, the Overys that lived down there, was going to Monticello that morning, and they asked if I'd like to ride along. We had to share rides in those days more than we do today. And so Morris said, "You'd better go because we don't have any Christmas for the children. Looks like it's gonna snow." Along the way over there it started snowing, and before we'd been there very long it just kept getting worse and worse.

I expect I had a dollar, but I wouldn't of had any more than that to spend on all their Christmas. We had to look to be sure what we wanted to spend it for, so I had paid twenty-five cents for a little lamp (your Mother's still got it today) with the colored base and all to it, with the little chimney. But I hadn't got anything for the boys yet. And Art came and said, "The snow's getting so bad, the roads are getting so bad we've got to go home right away." Well, we got up as far as the service station at Grugels at the edge of Wolcott, and I had to call the schoolhouse, 'cause my sister-in-law had asked me to help with some refreshments. She taught school in Wolcott, and she wanted to give some treats to her children that afternoon and she wanted me to help her. I had to call her from there, and the school was out. And so that was over.

Well, we started on to our house, and before we got there the roads got drifted so bad we had to get out of the car and leave it, and Bertha and Art had to walk on home. I went in, and I didn't have only the one Christmas present. And the weather was so bad, and we were so poor that Morris went out, your grandfather, and cut a branch off of an old snarly cedar tree out the front yard, and we stuck it in an old jar we used to make apple butter and put in — and stuck that down in there with some dirt. And the three children — Martha, John, and Jim (well, I don't think Jim was old enough to) — they popped some corn and strung it and decorated that little old branch. All we had through Christmas was the colored lamp for Martha. Those were the days!

The Biggest Christmas Present

Betty Williams
talking to Mike Faker

There's two things that I remember about the Depression that stuck with me — when I went to school I had to walk past my dad's blacksmith shop, and my shoes were beginning to look pretty bad. We kids were always able to go to the shoestore and pick out our own shoes. After school we would go to the shoestore and get some. The shoe man would know about what size we wore. So I stopped at the blacksmith shop and asked my dad if I could have the money for a new pair of shoes. He turned me down. He said, "Elizabeth, I just don't have the money." Now that broke my heart.

Then my uncle and aunt, they owned a grocery store — And my mother never drove a car (she never did know how to drive) so my uncle always delivered the groceries anyway, and my mother just called them in on the telephone, an order, and my uncle would always deliver them and put them on the back porch. Well, my dad was having a pretty big grocery bill, I mean it got up to around three or four hundred dollars of charged groceries, and we didn't know how we was ever going to get it paid. So my uncle and aunt, it was Christmas time, and they wanted my dad to start with a new slate, so they just wiped the grocery bill off and started a new grocery bill in January. Started from scratch. And that was the biggest Christmas present we ever had in the Depression!

Living in Town

Dorothea Wolfe
talking to Dave Moseley

My father, how shall I put this, had borrowed money on a farm, $600, with a land bank. And prices went to where you weren't getting anything for your grain and livestock. So instead of lose the farm for $600, he decided to sell it; and he sold it.

We had a property in town, and that was what we were left with. My father went to work for a man who raised seed corn for grain farming, but the people who bought the seed corn could not pay for it, so consequently things were rather touch-and-go. We had a home to live in, but you couldn't get cash you know. I mean there was no money coming in. I can remember my mom telling my father to give me ten cents to go to town to get a loaf of bread. Then he said, "I don't have ten cents."

We Lost Everything

Anonymous
talking to Donna Pierson

Ah! I can remember when the banks went broke. My dad was quite wealthy at the time. He owned farms in South Dakota, and Kentucky, and Indiana. I can remember him coming in after he'd been to the bank, and it closed right before he got there. He lost everything he had. And he finally had to get rid of part of the farms, and they didn't sell for but about five, fifteen, twenty dollars an acre, and then didn't get the money out of those, not the complete sum.

He kept the property in Kentucky that joined Fort Knox, and they started housekeeping down there, my mother an' dad did. Then they moved to Indiana before I was born. And I remember the prices of things when eggs were five cents a dozen and corn ten cents a bushel, and we farmed with horses. There wasn't any modern machinery back then, and you hand shucked the corn out of fields. I can remember when hamburger was three pounds for a quarter, bacon was three cents a pound, and people in the country raised most their food. My dad at one time traded a hog for a lot in Louisville, Kentucky, to a fella whose family was hungry. And everyone was in the same boat, no one had money.

The Blizzard of 1927

Alfred Bissonnette
talking to Brian Mathew

We did have some hard winters. We had some bitter winters, and probably not bein' fixed up as well as we are today to handle 'em, it made it much harsher then. The heat that we had in those days was probably not as good. The houses weren't as tight, and we noticed it. We didn't have central heat in a lot of the places. Now, fortunately, in our home we did have a furnace, and we heated with wood and cobs. We'd start the fire with cobs, and Dad would have to go down during the night and put wood on this furnace maybe a time or two to keep the fire all night. And we were very comfortable, but we didn't heat the total home like they do today.

We had blizzards back in those times same as we have now. Fact, I remember one blizzard, in 1927 it was, that we got caught at school. The busses got stuck tryin' to get there, and they come and got us with teams and wagons to take us home. We only lived a little over a mile, about a mile and a half it was, from the school, and that day it took us approximately three hours to get home with team and wagon. We were using two teams and two wagons, and we'd change often, breaking the trail trying to get through the snow drifts to get there. We finally made it, and some of the children that rode in this bus, in fact most of the neighbor children, they stayed at our place all night and

Contributed by Louise Ward

just gave up trying to get home at that time. So we did have those blizzards, but we didn't have the mechanical means to move this snow and everything that they have today.

In the next few days, as the weather began to clear and everything, the neighbors all got together, and to remove the snow from this road they did it by hand. They went out with scoopshovels and actually opened these roads out to the highway, which is U.S. 231 now. It was called the Jackson Highway at that time. It was a good stone road, but the side roads were mostly dirt roads. And so, we had our bad winters, and we had our good winters, same as we do today.

Hunting and Fishing

A listener cannot help but be struck by the incongruity of hearing so many stories of hunting and fishing in a place where every acre of tillable land is cultivated, where only a handful of hedgerows have been left standing, uprooted for a few extra feet of productive land, and where the fishing is done on small manmade lakes. But lifetime hunters like James (Lummy) Sheldon recall a time when a coon had a place to hide in the landscape and when abandoned houses provided warrens for animals. It was a time when men hunted for food and a few extra dollars. In his tales of the hunt, Lummy Sheldon tells of those who were close to him and who became closer in the practice and perfection of their demanding craft. The hunt, as Lummy Sheldon makes clear, was not an escape from the community, but its intensification—and here in his story the fathers and sons who appear elsewhere in this volume telling their individual tales are joined in a common pursuit.

Coon Hunting

James Sheldon
talking to Carol Burke

Started out coon hunting when I was about twelve or thirteen years old. I was from Monon, and a man named Jake up there gave me a real red bone hound, a registered one with papers with who tied the pup on it. I got an old hunter that I used to hunt with when I was a kid, and I said, "You train this dog for me." He had a dog, and he took the dogs out and his dog treed a skunk. Mine wouldn't go near it. This man had a big rifle, and he shot my dog. And so that put me out of business for awhile. Then I got another dog, and ever since, I've had dogs, had one to thirty ever since.

I had a cousin of mine from Chicago, and Jack Murray was his name. He had never been with a dog. I bought a black and tan dog, and that dog seemed like every time of day and night he wanted to tree a skunk. So we was up on the river one night, and the dog was running the track. All

Contributed by White County Historical Society

74

at once I heard him panting. I said to Jack, "You take this lantern and run in there to the little pond (the pond was dried up). You take this lantern now and run and help that dog kill that coon." Because I said I didn't think he could do it, boy, he took that lantern and club and went over in there. He just ran in there right quick to help the dog, and the dog had a skunk. When Jack came out of there his old coattail was sticking right straight out. Boy! Was he ever going! I knew the dog had a skunk because that was all he treed was skunks. Oh, we had a lot of fun!

One night I took my wife with me. There was a truck over on Route 231, we heard when it backfired. She thought that they were shooting, and she took off back to the car. She'd liked to have torn her clothes off getting through the fence to get back into the car. And she hasn't been hunting since.

You asked about the best time for coon hunting. Well, sometimes early in the fall is a real good time. And then maybe the weather will get bad, and they'll be held up for a long time, and they won't come down. A snow will come or something like that. When that snow melts, why then they'll come down and go running. Then you can really have a lot of fun running after them. They'll get hungry, and then they'll want to come down and get something to eat.

You'll be walking down along the ditches and see any of their tracks, why, that's where you aim to head for. You get where there's a timber, where there's a lot of them trees in it. Why, that's the best place to go. Like in the country around here, you just get stragglers traveling up the ditches, but get where there's a lot of them trees, why, then you can generally have pretty good luck hunting coon. You get up along the Iroquois River and can have a good time up there. If it rains and the water gets high you can't get around it and back in on the bayous.

Joe Cook and I have been up there when you couldn't get back there at all. And then we've been up there when the ice was on. Joe was up there on one side and didn't want to come across on my side. Joe didn't come across because he thought the ice would break. But my dog had been running the track and crossed on the other side, treed a coon over there, and Joe shot it. I said, "Joe, that's my coon." So he said, "OK, I'll throw it across to you." So he threw it across, and his dog came over and got it and took it back. Joe said, "I guess he wants me to have it," and away he went with it.

You asked what a good coon dog is. Well, it's one that will bark trees. You can get a lot of them to run coons, but you can't get them to bark them. If you get a dog that will bark trees, don't matter what breed it is — black bone, red bone, tan, collie as far as that goes — when a coon goes up the tree they'll just go and bark it. That's the main thing. I've had cur dogs that was a good coon dog if you ever went to the woods with them. And I've had some of the most beautiful dogs that wasn't worth a dime. You take them out, and if they come back and lay down beside you, they ain't too good.

If a dog is scratched up and his ears have been torn from fighting coons, that's a good sign. That's about the only way you can tell one unless you take him out and try it. I've had so many of them. I'd trade for and buy one and the fellow would say they were a number one coon dog, and you would take it out. The other dogs would be running the track, and look around and there curled up behind you asleep is this dog. So it's just hard to tell. Some of the poorest looking dogs make the best coon dogs.

My dad was a hunter. He went out with the barber, who used to be up here at Goodland, and run fox. They were old fox hunters, see. He didn't really like coon hunting, though. I remember one night we talked him into going hunting, and we went down south to where there was a hedgerow, see. We had a couple of young pups and didn't know what the pups would run. They got after a coon and were pushing that coon pretty hard. The coon was out in a corn field, and he was coming back in. My dad was standing there. No light or nothing. And this coon was getting pretty close to him. The coon was wanting someplace to go up, so, he went right up my dad and scratched the devil out of him, scratched his face and everything else. Figured he was a tree, he did. He thought that my dad was a stump or something, I guess. He went right up the old man and scratched the devil out of him. Man, he never went hunting much with us after that.

But we went on hunting coon for years. We would skin them. We'd put them on a wide board on the side of a building. Take hundreds of nails to stretch a coon hide. Just rip him up the belly and stretch him out flat, see. Here in the last seven or eight years, why, the coons have been skinned like a muskrat. Now they just open the legs and peel the hide down and put it on a stretcher. But in them days, you tried to get your coon as square as you could make it.

After you made sure the skin had dried good you would ship it to some fur company. There were several companies you could use—Silverman's, and Sears and Roebuck started to buy a lot of them. For years here my brother and I hunted together, and we managed to run around fifty. We worked pretty hard sometimes. Sometimes we'd get fifty and maybe the next season forty-nine. For six seasons straight we run about forty-nine, fifty, maybe fifty-one. We had a pretty decent pair of dogs, see.

We used to sell the whole coon for seventy-five cents, and last year the grandkids got fifty dollars for a big coon. I see a lot of differences now from what it was when I was young. Years ago, when I was a young lad, we skinned everything and shipped it. That was about the only way you had to get rid of it, see. There was fur companies sent you a price list and tags to ship to them. All you had to do was wrap it up in a burlap bag and put the tags on it and mail it to them, which was a good deal far as that was concerned. But there have been a lot of changes since then. They went through and cut a lot of timber out. It used to be, around here, years ago, the timber was so thick you could just get in a car. You could always find a good place to catch coon. Well, they put new roads through, and everyone of these new roads went right through the best hunting territory there was, see. And then they got to cleaning ditches and cutting all the trees down, and there aren't any places for the coons to put up. There used to be empty houses, and then they got to burning the houses around here. Had two or three houses around here where there was coons, and you could go over there any night. Just go over there and turn the dogs out, and the coons would be out feeding and they would come out from under the houses. The dogs would maybe run around and bring them up a tree or back under the porch. If you didn't get them one night, you'd come back the next. But they burnt up all them houses, and there is hardly anyplace for the coons to put up.

Hunting for Profit

William Sheldon
talking to Don Sheldon

For hunting we all had either a club, or one guy carried a single barrel shotgun, 'cause you didn't waste any shells. At night we didn't carry a gun to shoot coon or anything out of a tree. You had to climb up and shake 'em out, and the dogs had to kill 'em from there on. At the price, you couldn't afford to shoot 'em, 'cause the shells cost more than the skins were worth. A coon, if he was a good big one, brought you a dollar. If he was a small one, he brought you fifty cents. A skunk would bring you maybe fifty cents and a possum, well, that was ten cents. And then there was a bounty; they paid for crows and hawks in them days. Crows feet, if you got a pair of crows feet, they was worth five cents a piece. That's what we spent our time at for relaxation. Trapping and hunting like that, and maybe for the whole winter, if you was lucky, you might get fifteen cents back for all your trouble.

Selling Rabbits

Earl Honeywell
talking to Marc Deardorff

We had a bounty on rabbits. You'd get five cents a pair for every pair of rabbit ears, and that kept me in spending money. And I bought a little twenty-two-caliber rifle, a little Stevens rifle. I got that rifle by gathering up buffalo bones. Now what'd they use buffalo bones for? In that day they'd gather bones of buffaloes, steers, animals of that kind, and the bones were used in the purification of sugar. That was the basis for purifying sugar, and so I gathered up these bones. I don't know what I got, but anyway I got a sufficient number of bones that I bought me a little twenty-two rifle from Sears and Roebucks. It cost me two dollars and twenty-five cents. Then I didn't have enough money to buy shells, cartridges. So I had to borrow money from my mother, and with a quarter I got one hundred cartridges, two boxes. Now that was the beginning.

Then after that my mother saw that I was doing a pretty good job. I was bringing in a lot of rabbits. We had to. That was a source of food. And also the rabbits were eating us out of home you might say. I've seen 'em eat hay stacks right down. We had to do something with rabbits and so I would shoot a lot of rabbits. And that's the way in which I got that rifle over there in the corner — with rabbit ears.

Contributed by Richard Wheeler

They Were So Thick

Gerald Forbes
talking to Matt Lile

Now you mentioned hunting rabbits. At one time I went across the road when we had about, oh, two foot of snow, and there was an old orchard about a half mile east. And I only had, I think, some two or three shells for the gun, and I shot those rabbits. And those rabbits were so thick around in the bushes and so forth that I just went to hittin' them with the end of the gun barrel!

Hunting at Recess

Anonymous
talking to Marcia Furrer

We went to a little country school, and we often used to have to walk a mile to school back in them days. Our spending money came from hunting, and usually all the boys at noon, over the noon hour, we would get one of the boys' dogs to chase up the rabbits, and we would go out with billy clubs and catch the rabbits and skin them and divide them up. Or we'd catch any other game that we could maybe sell furs off of.

But this one time we got a surprise. We was going out across country, and we came across a farmer's haystack. We seen some holes going in there, and we thought, hey, maybe we could get some rabbits. He had left a fork laying there, so we got the fork and started digging, but to our surprise out came a skunk, and of course he got all of us. At that time skunk furs were real good, too, so we was going to skin him, but we took him back to the schoolhouse. Well, we didn't know what to do with him, so we just stuck him under the schoolhouse until after school was out. We was kind of dumb because we already had the smell on our clothes, and we brought this right into the schoolhouse with us, and our teacher made us hang all of our clothes out on the barbwired fence. That was about the end of our hunting game.

The Colored People Who Fished for Carp

Irene Schmitz
talking to Tony Anderson

Oh boy, I've seen my dad bring home the big fish! He didn't have to tell it; he'd bring home and show them to us. In the river down here, up until about fifteen to twenty years ago, they used to get real good fish. They'd get wall-eyed pike, bass, croppie, bluegill, a few catfish, bullheads, and carp, of course. But my dad, I think, and my uncle both caught two of the largest wall-eyed pike out here at the river, as far as they know, south of town. My dad's weighed over six pounds, and I think Bert's weighed seven some pounds. They hardly ever went fishing when they didn't bring home a nice mess of good edible fish. Fishing was really something in those days. And a lot of people fished. We used to go to the river, and a lot of the colored people from Gary and Hammond would come down here, south of Brook here, and fish by the river bridge. Well, my dad would catch carp, and of course they didn't like carp so they would throw them back. The colored people would be on the other side of the river, and they'd say, "Oh, don't throw those in the river. We want them." And my dad says, "Well, I'm glad you told me, because I'll save them for you." So every time he'd catch a carp he'd put it on a stringer, and sometimes he'd have a long stringer of carp. The colored people would leave before we would, and they would come across the river on the bridge and pick them up. Once I asked one of the colored women, I said, "How do you prepare the fish." She said, "Well, you smoke them." You put them in a brine water for awhile to keep them real cold. Then they're drained out of that. Then they smoke them like you do in a barbecue pit or something. She said they're very, very good. I've never tried them so I don't know if they were or not. But they liked them, so we never threw them away. We always give them to them.

The Ten-and-a-Half Pound Northern

Jerry Cook
talking to Stan Cook

Another boy and I, we were sixteen. He was from Chicago. Our parents had one boat out with the good equipment, and he and I took the other boat. We'd go back around the corner in this lake, and it so happened there's a nice set of buildings there, and this guy who owned it had some nice looking granddaughters who'd be up there waterskiing. We got used of always going back there, not getting our fishing poles wet, just sitting there with binoculars watching the girls. We went back, and we sort of fished by the way. We were trolling along, and Bob says, "Hold it. Shut the motor off. I've snagged something." Figured we'd caught weeds on the bottom so we stopped, and he tried to work his pole, and pulled gently and cranked and pulled and cranked. He said, "It's coming in." He kept working it slowly, and it floated to the top. We looked back, and he did have something. Up towards the top floated some weeds, and in amongst the weeds we saw this head with two eyeballs. This kid about went wild. We didn't want to make a lot of noise or racket, and just keep the line tight. He stayed on top of the water, and we had one net in the boat. It was one that had real little thin strings and holes in it because we didn't expect to catch many fish. Mom and Dad had the good net, and here we had one with holes in it. We know if we tried to get that fish in that net he would tear the net apart and get away. So I stood up in the boat with the net in my hands waving because there were people a half mile to a mile away fishing. I was trying to get their attention to come over and bring us a net. Nobody did. Nobody ever did see us there. He kept reeling in slowly, and that fish got up near the boat, and we knew that we had to do something. I knew I had one shot at him, or one stab at him. You don't normally catch a fish from behind. You have to dip him from the front and come in from behind, and the net catches his tail while he takes off. So I waited while he got right up by the boat, and I dipped under him real quick and was able to get him in the front end and throw him on the floor of the boat. This kid jumped up and down on top of him, and he was just hysterical. He sat on that fish all the way into camp, which was about three miles. He'd look at the fish real slimy and just bust out laughing and laughing and laughing, and he'd quit laughing and get real serious, and look at the fish and start laughing and laughing. We got it up to shore, and it was a ten-and-a-half-pound northern. He was really tickled and proud of it.

Food

When asked to recall a pleasant time, many people told about the social occasions surrounding food: neighbors getting together to harvest, to butcher, or just for an evening's entertainment of taffy pulling.

Getting Off the Mission List

Ruth Humphreys
talking to John Lemming

We were a mission church. We were a poor church. We never yet have been too affluent, but we're not a mission church. But we were then, and Mrs. Bada Stockston one day called the women together, and she said, "Would you like to be rid of this mission business at the church?" And we all said, "Yes." She said, "Well, I've had an idea. Why don't we serve thrashing dinners down here in the basement of our church?" We'd had our church made over, and we had a nice basement in it, and we had two old range cook stoves, or we got two when we decided to do this. And so we all said yes, we'd be willing to do it.

So we went down there, and we would go early in the morning and peel several bushel of potatoes and roast all the meat. The man would bring it out from the meat market for us, and we would make pies at home. We served those dinners for twenty-five cents a meal. And it just kept getting so more and more runs would come for us till we were serving more than a hundred people. Everybody was busy, and don't think they weren't! My job was to mash potatoes. Verna Sturdon and I mashed all those potatoes, and I've still got the old potato masher hanging here on my fireplace that I used, with the long handle. That was a regular thing, and the children all looked forward to that. They played in the sand. Meadowlake Church is on a sand hill. We all took our children with us, and the children played in the sand and made all sorts of castles, farms, and everything else while we worked in the basement, and we just—everybody worked—and we just got along fine. We took ourselves off that mission list, and we've never been a mission church since.

Thrashing Dinners

Ceil Schafer
talking to Beverly Kenoyer

We'd get up at three in the morning, and this would be so we could get the work all done before the men would come, because we would have three men for breakfast. These three men, one of them was the water hauler, one was the separator man, and one was the engineer. For our thrashing dinner there would be like thirty men, and then the neighbor ladies would come and help with the meal, and of course the children would be there. Our table was set with a white tablecloth. You might be interested to know that we didn't have anything much to get rid of flies — and so there would be no flies in the house, we would take a branch from a tree and shoo the flies out.

Then our daddy would get up early of a morning. About five o'clock in the morning he would go to town and get the meat for the dinner. That would be about eighteen pounds of roast beef. There was no chickens. We didn't have any chickens big enough to fry, so we couldn't have fried chicken. So then they would get five pounds of cold meat (which was pressed ham) and three pounds of cheese and about five loaves of bread. We would churn our own butter, and we would make about seven or eight pies; and there would be two cakes we would bake. If you would like to hear what our menu was like: roast beef, gravy, mashed potatoes, coleslaw. We'd get prunes and cook those. They'd have dried peaches cooked, green beans, sliced cucumbers, sliced tomatoes. If we had turnips we'd cook some of those. There would be lemonade, water, and coffee. Our cake was a white cake. It'd have pink icing on it with some coconut sprinkled on it. Our yellow cakes would have white icing. When they got all finished with their thrashing, they'd have a thrashing meeting then. Your grandpa Bevie was secretary of that, and he did all the figuring for this. Then the ladies would bake cakes, and then they would have ice cream.

Hog Butchering

Anonymous
talking to Betty Miller

You butchered your own meat. Now you didn't go into the grocery store and buy five pounds of hamburger or something. I can remember us like butchering six to eight hogs at a time, and this again was a neighborhood get-together. There would be several farmers who would go together, and, say, they would butcher one week at one farmer's house and the next week at another farmer's house. I might explain a little bit on how that butchering was done. You started out early òf a morning with several iron kettles. The large type was about, oh, thirty inches in diameter. Fill those full of water and build a big wood fire around 'em to heat 'em. It would have to be started early 'cause the water had to be boiling to process these hogs. The hogs were killed, and then they were brought onto — They usually set up some kind of platform for scraping the hogs. This was often done with an A-frame where you could hoist the hogs up and down into a tank of water. A common thing was a fifty-five-gallon drum with the end cut out. It would have enough water in it that when you sub-

Contributed by the Indiana State Library, Indiana Division Picture Collection

merged the hog he would get scalded all over, so you could scrape the hair off of them. And then they would take the intestines out of them and save them. They would clean those, and that is where you stuff your sausage. It's quite an operation. Then the hogs can be cut up so you would have your hams, your shoulders, your pork chops. Some of these people were very good at different phases of it. As an example, there would be someone of the group who would make the sausage. He'd pick out all the different meat and grind them up into sausage. One thing that was real tricky was how to season sausage. Sausage was seasoned with salt, pepper, and sage if you like sage. Then you would grind this sausage and put it into the clean casings. One thing that was popular with sausage was to fry this sausage and put it in a four- or five-gallon stone jar. Then they would heat lard and pour it on it. If you had a cool cellar you could keep that and have sausage pretty late in the year.

You would also sugar-cure the hams and shoulders so you could preserve it without refrigeration. The hams and shoulders would be covered with a mixture of brown sugar, red pepper, black pepper, and salt. Each farmer had his own so-called recipe that they used. The meat would then be covered with newspaper and then wrapped in white cloth, usually cloths that they had gotten feed in or supplement. And those are what was used around the meat. Something I might tell you about this. If you never seen a sugar-cured ham — they are very delicious. But some things happen to them that in today's modern technology we don't expect. There's a mold forms on that meat, and it looks real green. If you first saw it you'd think it was spoiled, but if you got the proper cure, it wouldn't be. In other words, you might be butchering in the spring while it was freezing weather in February and March when a lot of the butchering was done. And in June, July, and August you'd be eating some of this meat, and it would be hanging out in the real hot weather with no refrigeration. And it was worked out very well.

They also rendered their lard, and this was quite an operation. This lard was cooked in these kettles after they'd heated the water to scald the hogs and clean the kettles out. They would put the fat meat in. They would cut it up into small chunks, like about one-inch cubes. And when it was cooked and done, you'd have lard. Also, this lard would have to be squeezed out. And that's where they got what they call cracklins. And these were very delicious. They would save those as something you could eat a little later. You needed lard to cook with. It wouldn't be uncommon to have a, oh, I think the lard cans were probably fifty-pound cans. We'd have six or eight cans of lard to run us for our cooking purposes for the next year.

Curing Meat

Ceil Schafer
talking to Beverly Kenoyer

I have a recipe for curing meat. That is two cups of salt, one cup of brown sugar, two tablespoons of black pepper and one tablespoon of red pepper. You mix this all together and rub it on the meat real good, especially around the bone. Meat will start spoiling around the bone quicker if you don't get enough salt to the bone. This is put into a paper bag. You put this meat in a paper bag "like the pig walked," with the bone down, and this was hung up. Then after it cured you could use it just any time.

Apple Hill

Bessie Hackley
talking to Lisa Kruger

We buried most of our apples. We'd put a layer of straw on the ground, put boards on top of the straw, then we'd pile the apples on it, and then a lot of straw on top. Then we'd dig a trench around the outer edge. Then we'd put dirt over that. We would make a trench around it and throw the dirt over. Then along in the winter, after we'd used up the apples we'd stored in the basement, we'd pull a board out and reach in and get fresh apples out of these apples that were put underneath the dirt. Of course, they were clean because they were covered with straw and kept real clean. The trench that was dug around it drained the water off, so that if it got muddy and snowy, why, there wouldn't be any water get in the apples. We would have them last until — Sometimes it would be warm weather before we'd be getting out of apples. We used apples in our lunch pails and had apples on the table to piece on when we got home from school.

Early Refrigeration, I

Anonymous
talking to Betty Miller

Well, back in those days some people did not have a refrigerator. I can remember that for the early refrigerator we dug a hole in the backyard and would put a tile down in the yard. That would hold the temperature of the ground. We'd put perishable goods in there. That was very limited, but one of the things we did use it for was butter. That was always stored out there — so if you wanted butter for lunch or breakfast or any meal you'd have to go to the tile that was buried and get the butter.

They also had a lot of springs, and they had spring houses where they kept milk, butter, this type of stuff. But we milked twice a day, so there wasn't the problem of refrigerating the milk.

The other thing that was popular was to dig a hole in the ground and put apples in it and cabbage. Some potatoes could even go into this. Onions could. Then you covered it back up with a layer of soil on top, and the ground would freeze during the winter. Then you would break open a small place in it, and that would be your fruit cellar. That was right out in the garden. You only kept a small hole so you could reach in, and you had to place your stuff so that you could get to it from that one hole so you didn't get your whole thing broke open.

Early Refrigeration, II

Evelyn Sheldon
talking to Don Sheldon

We didn't have ice and things to refrigerate our butter and things; we had a cistern. It was my job to go out and take the lid off the cistern. The butter would be hanging down in a little bucket on a chain. I'd have to pull the chain up and the bucket, because that was the only way of keeping our butter from spoiling.

At that time we didn't have any icebox. Later on, when we did live in town, we had an icebox, and the town pleasure was to follow the ice wagon down the street and see if you could have a little hunk of ice when he chipped it for different people to take in. Sometimes we had the money for ice, and sometimes we didn't.

Fresh Fish

Eva Talley
talking to Ellen Goad, Sally Waymire, Roger Emond, Tony Anderson, and Peggy Mormann

The pond back of our house — When the river got up, fish filled the pond so all the uncles and cousins would come with their seines, and they would get fish for the whole neighborhood. And they'd just get enough for however long they could keep them. Then they would come back again. But of course the water gradually went down, and when it was about to all get out — There was a ditch that led to the river, but they kept a wire over that ditch as long as there was water in the pond so the fish couldn't get out and they could have fish. But when it was about to go down to the point where they would have to let the fish go back to the river, my father would bring quite a quantity of them to a tank that he had built in the front yard. After we had

Contributed by Sandra Longest

got a windmill that pumped the water, he built this great big concrete basin. There was a spray like a fountain that filled it, and it kept full of water. So he put the fish in this fountain, and he fed them, and as we needed fish we would take the fish out of that and have them. So we could have fish practically — well, a good part of the summer at least. That was the way they managed their food. We always managed to use the food that was available.

Taffy Pulls

Ruth Provo
talking to Deb Behrens

We'd get together. Some of our relatives would come over a lot of times, and my dad would make this taffy. I don't know just the exact amounts that he would take of the molasses and water. I remember him boiling this down to a soft ball (when he'd drop it in water). Anyway, he knew just about when it would be ready, he'd made so much of it.

When it got to the soft ball stage he would pour it out in these big platters like, grease them you know, and let them cool. You could pick it up and it'd be stiff like. But they didn't always let it get real cold. They'd just let it get cooled off real good to where it wouldn't burn their hands. Then you had to grease your hands and flour your hands and pull the taffy. We'd pull it back and forth. There'd be two of you. Then you'd pull it back and forth and lap it over, get ahold of it and pull it back and forth. It'd be like a big rope going back and forth.

It was real good. After they pulled it so long — till it got real light colored and satiny — then they'd stretch it out on the table till it got real long, like a big rope. They'd let it lay there just awhile, then they'd take a knife and crack it every so far apart.

We never bought candy. Never. He always made all of our candy. We didn't have it too often. It was mostly at Christmas and the Fourth of July. Of course, he would make it before that. We made more in the wintertime, like for Christmas and New Year's, because usually in the summer they would be busy in the fields.

Dad was the candy maker. And he'd make homemade root beer. He got him a capper and got the bottles. At the Fourth of July then, we'd always have a party with homemade ice cream and root beer. We had a tank out where our well pumped water into it, a big tank. Dad would put that down in there, leave the caps on it and set it down in there, and let the water pump in there to get it cold, and it'd be real cold.

Snow Cream

Lydia McDonald
talking to Chris Annis

We had snow cream. We'd take real clean snow just after it first fell, just before it got dirty, and we'd take milk and flavor it with vanilla and sugar and pour it over the snow. And we thought it was real good. You had to be sure the snow was clean because it gets dirty pretty quick. We thought that was quite a treat!

Hominy and Sauerkraut

Esther Strasburger
talking to Tom Flora

My mother would always make a big batch of hominy with lye. Then she'd have to wash it and wash it to get the lye off, and also to get the little eyes out of the corn, but it was really good. And then in the wintertime my father would roll in that big barrel of sauerkraut that they had made in the fall. It'd be frozen, and he had put lots of leaves of cabbage on top, so he would take all that off, and then we'd all stand around and eat that frozen cabbage and slaw. Was that ever good! It's a wonder it didn't kill us, but it didn't hurt us.

Recipe for Lye Soap

Ceil Schafer
talking to Beverly Kenoyer

Here is one for homemade lye soap, and this is what we used when we washed on a washboard. We used that for a long, long time, until they came out with detergents, and then we didn't use quite as much.

That was six pounds of fat melted, two and a half pints of hot water and one can lye. Dissolve the lye in the hot water, let cool. Then pour lye solution in a slow, easy stream into the melted fat, stirring constantly. Continue stirring until cool. Pour into boxes that have been dipped into cold water. Cut in desired size of squares when cold and set.

Remedies, Beliefs, and Names

Everyone we interviewed told us at least one remedy or superstition, and most could recall how a person or a place got its name. They told of the treatments of buttonweed, fat meat, and vinegar stew. They cautioned against cutting hair in the dark of the moon. They told about Voodoo Crossing and the school called Never Fail. These bits of lore flourished in a time when people, in the absence of official expertise, concocted their own cures for the common ailments and predicted the weather by the signs.

Colds, I

George Scott
talking to Peggy Mormann

It was a common thing. When someone had a bad cold or flu, they used to make a vinegar stew. It was not really a delicacy. But what it is — You take a pie tin or some flat dish and fill it with vinegar, and then you put in it all the vinegar you can find. Then of course, you heat it, and you make it as hot as you can. Then you eat it. You don't want to eat too much. But it's supposed to make you sweat a lot, and that was supposed to be good for a cold. I tasted it, and it's not the best.

Of course, if you had a sore throat, you usually wore a flannel cloth around your neck with some type of compound on that cloth. A lot of kids wore that to school all the time, and you always knew who had a sore throat or a cold. Their chest was greased. You'd always spot them around the room.

Colds, II

Irene Schmitz
talking to Tony Anderson

Well, my mother, when we had bad colds in the winter, would take a piece of wool flannel squares and put it across our chest. And she would heat up menthol oil and soak that and lay it on our chest, then pin it inside of our night clothes. Or she made what they called onion poultices.

They would take onions, peel and slice them, and fry them in oil. Then they would mash them up, and they would put them between cloths, two squares of cloths, and then they would put a paper over the top of it (like squares of newspaper) and fasten that in your clothes. If you had a real bad chest cold, they used it. It was warm, and I think that's what the remedy was that really helped. But maybe the oil penetrated. I don't know for sure, but you had to lay flat on your back, because it was a kind of greasy mess.

Then my mother used to make what they called onion syrup. She'd cut up a nice white onion in small chunks and put it in a granite pie pan and sprinkle sugar all over it, stir it up. We had a base burner for a heater, and it had a floor board much like the modern stoves did have. She'd put the pan on top of the floor board under the stove. It was real sweet, and it would make a nice plump syrup. Then when we had a cold, she'd give us a spoonful of that, and it didn't taste too bad.

Colds, III

Lillian Allie
talking to Cheryl McCollum

They had to fix up their own medicine. You couldn't find a doctor all the time; you couldn't get to them! They had, like, colds on their lungs; that's what they called "Lung Fever." They had colds or something like that, and they'd use 'em a goose grease and mix that with turpentine and camphor or something to rub on them, you know.

Then sometimes I used to hear my mother say, too, that when children had that cold in their lungs, they'd cut strips off sacks, old brown sacks and spread (and put), oh, mustard and all kinds of stuff on it. I had to wear 'em, and they was so scratchy and so hot it nearly drove us crazy. And they used an herb called ginseng, and my father used to go to the woods and dig it. In them years they used to get two dollars and fifty cents a pound for it.

Stomachache

Earl York
talking to Kent Claton

For the old-fashion stomachache, they take 'em to a doctor now. Why, Gramma would just go out and get some button weeds and make a tea out of it, and we had to drink that. And that was worse than a bellyache.

Stomachache and Stone Bruises

Anonymous
talking to Donna Pierson

We used to get peppermint from a stream nearby, wild peppermint, and my mother would boil that and make tea for stomachaches. For stone bruises she'd use sweet cream and mashed peach tree leaves.

Earache

Sue Sutton
talking to Rhonda Sutton

If you had an earache, they used to blow smoke in your ear. That was supposed to cure the headache, or the earache.

Asthma

Clara Lawson
talking to Jackie Meadors

A lady in the neighborhood who was like a witch doctor, she had a lot of remedies. She claimed she could cure a child with asthma. A neighbor boy had it, and she stood him by a maple tree and pulled up a lock of hair out of his head. She twisted it around nine times and pushed the hair into the bark of the tree. When the hair could not be seen, she said, he would be cured.

The Itch

Ruth Humphreys
talking to John Lemming

Well, we had a remedy for the itch. My brother came in town one Saturday night. Martha and Jim—we all pretty near had the itch. They had got it at school, and he called up from town and said he'd heard that if you'd put carbolic acid, I believe it was, in some water and bathe them that it would cure that itch. So we made two pans of it, and we put a kid in each tub and bathed them in that. And did they scream and bawl! And I'm pretty sure that it was carbolic acid that we used. Anyway, it burned like the dickens!

Contributed by White County Historical Society

Infection, I

Sam Gruber
talking to Susan Getz

I remember stepping onto a rusty nail, and back in them days we believed in herbs. We took this smartweed when it was about knee high. We'd take a whole bunch of it, and we'd boil it. Then I'd put my foot — put it in that boiling water — that smartweed tea. That smartweed just colored the water so nice brown, and I put my foot in there, and it'd take all the poison out. Put it in there as hot as I could stand it.

Infection, II

Paul Roby
talking to Pam Kyburz

We used fat meat to draw out the poison. We'd just take a piece of fat meat, put it on the sore, and that would draw it out.

Infection, III

Bessie Hackley
talking to Lisa Kruger

The hired men would chew tobacco. If they had a bad cut, or stepped on a nail, or got hurt with a pitchfork, or something like that, they would chew the tobacco and get it all moist and put it on as a poultice. That was one remedy.

Infection, IV

Jane Packard
talking to Bryan Dunbar

The strangest remedy that I ever heard of was one that came from a person that lived about a mile from our house. She was visiting my mother one afternoon when I was sitting with my foot up because I had stepped on a rusty nail, and it was sort of red. My mother was concerned about it. This lady said that she should take the nail and rub it with grease and hang it up in the garage. Hang it up someplace, and that was supposed to take care of the inflamed foot.

To Draw Thorns

Ed Kyburz
talking to Sandy Kyburz

I can remember one time when I run a hedge thorn in my foot, and I walked around for a whole week with crutches. We couldn't get that hedge thorn out. My dad said to me at the breakfast table one morning, and said to Eddie, "When you get breakfast ate you get the pony and go out in the pasture and follow them cows around. Whenever a cow has a bowel movement you put a little shovelful of that in a five pound salt sack (they were cloth sacks in them days), and you come home and put your foot in that, and you walk around with that." And that's what I did for about two days, and that thorn came out. And that was a cure to draw thorns.

Poison

Ruth Humphreys
talking to John Lemming

This one time, why, Uncle John had a go-cart. He was little — I can't remember if it was Uncle John or Uncle Jim — anyway I had him in a go-cart, and I was out in the back yard under a tree that was out there. And so I was leaving Ruth and Martha to watch him, and I went across the road to work in the garden. Had a garden across the road that year, and I had an old daisy fly killer. But you don't know what that is. That was a thing that was made out of metal and about six inches long and five inches wide, and it had daisy flowers on it. In each one of the centers of those daisies' flower would be poison to kill flies. There was a place where you'd pour water in there that made sweet water come up on those daisies and kill the flies.

I put some sugar on those daisies, and the minute it was out of my mouth I knew I had said the wrong thing. I said, "Now don't you girls lick the sugar off the daisy fly killer." I went on over to the garden. I knew I shouldn't have said it, and just a little bit Ruth said, "Martha's licked all the sugar off the daisy fly killer!" Oh, my land! I went back, and I called up my mother-in-law here in town. She said, "Oh my goodness, Ruth, you've got to get her to throw up." And so she called up Doc Spencer and told him what had happened. Says she's got to throw up. Anything, she's got to throw up. Well, in a little bit — In those days when the telephone rang everybody's telephone rang, and you could take the receiver down and listen. And Mrs. Overy had listened and she heard that, and Bessie Long who lived on down the road there where Musall's live today, she heard it, and both of them were running down the road to our house. And your grandpa was out in the field, and he seen those people running. He jumped off and left the mules standing right in the middle of the field hitched to the corn plow and run up to the house to see what was the matter. And there we was with Martha. We couldn't

104

make her throw up. I melted lard. I give her raw egg. I give her vinegar with something in it and everything. Finally, we were so desperate, and she just would not throw up. She just drank all that, but she wouldn't throw up. We had a swing in the tree there in the back yard, and Grandpa put her in that swing and twisted her all up just as tight as he could. Then he let her go and let her untwist herself. And brother! She heaved! And was we all relieved. Oh, yes, we had plenty of excitement.

A Navel That Won't Heal

Sue Sutton
talking to Rhonda Sutton

And a baby when it's navel wouldn't heal right, they would sew a silver dollar in a band and put it around the baby so the silver dollar rested over the navel, and that was supposed to heal it right.

Warts, I

Thelma Long
talking to Jill DeSplinter

I had a whole bunch of warts on my hand. I went to my grandma's one time, and they told me to go in and get the dishrag when Grandma wasn't lookin' and wipe my hands on it and go out and bury it. I did, and my warts went away. When the dishrag rotted, why, that was when my warts went away.

Warts, II

James Sheldon
talking to Carol Burke

They had all kinds of sayings for warts. If you take an ear of corn, rub it on the warts, and then throw it over your shoulder—if the hogs ate the ear of corn then the wart would go away.

I had cousins that had warts, and they come out home once and said that somebody told them to rub ears of corn on the warts and throw it into your relations' hogs. If they eat it, the warts will leave. I guess it must have worked, 'cause they haven't got the warts anymore.

Warts, III

Sue Sutton
talking to Rhonda Sutton

If you had a wart you would rub a penny on it and put the penny in the Bible. Yes, the wart went away. I don't know if it's putting the penny in the Bible; it would go away.

To Stop Bleeding

Sam Gruber
talking to Susan Getz

I have a story I'll never forget as long as I live. That's when I was on a horse, and I drove a couple of cows out to a pasture, to another pasture. In that pasture was a big bull. I drove these cows in that pasture, and I went to whirl it around to go home. When I got off the horse to open the gate, this bull come up, and he gored my horse and threw this horse up in the air. He had horns that was eight inches long, sharp as a needle, and he run his horn, this horn, into the front chest between the front legs of that horse.

Every other step that that horse took a cup of blood would shoot out there. And I had to go a quarter of a mile to the closest house, and there I went to the barn. Didn't say anything to the neighbor, went right in the barn. I was acquainted with these people, and I got the cobwebs down from inside of the ceiling and the bottom of the barn. With an old broomstick I got all of these cobwebs. I got a burlap sack, and I took and found some twine and tied each corner of the gunny sack. I tied it around his neck to get that blood clotted, to keep the horse from bleeding to death 'cause I had another half mile to go home. And he lived. But, you know, that was the best horse before that. It didn't make any difference if the calves or the cattle wouldn't move. I'd say, "Bite 'em," and I'd spur him a little bit, and he'd get 'em going. But after the bull horned him he never was any good anymore. The minute a steer would turn a little bit, he would dodge. He was afraid they'd come after him again. He was no good then anymore to drive cattle.

Sore Shoulder on a Horse

Dan Reel
talking to Jerry Cook

We used to take salt water and wash the shoulders off. Dad said that'd make their shoulder tough so they didn't get such sore shoulders.

But us three boys found we didn't have no horses with sore shoulders. Dad didn't hardly have any that didn't have. He always thought you had to have a pad under the collar. See, that was the worst thing you could have.

We had one horse that we bought that had sores on his collar. And they had what they called a "humane collar." It was stuffed with some kind of medical stuff. Put that on him. And that didn't cure him so we just took and cut holes where them sores was and stuffed it with wool so the other stuff wouldn't come off. We healed him up. After that we just put a straight collar on him just tight enough so you could stick your fingers in.

Cutting Hair, I

Hugh Jackson
talking to Denise Dotson

Back when I was a kid, a lot of the old timers, they wouldn't have their hair cut in March. They just wouldn't. No, your hair wouldn't grow right from then on.

Cutting Hair, II

Dan Reel
talking to Jerry Cook

You cut your hair in the dark of the moon, it won't grow as fast as when the moon's agrowin'.

On New Year's Day

Glenn Meadors
talking to Dave Phillips

I won't cut my fingernails on Sunday. That's bad luck. Now my wife won't pay any attention to it.

We always have cabbage on New Year's Day. You'll have money the rest of the year. We've always managed to have a couple of dollars between one New Year's and the next. One time we got down to two and a quarter. While my mother was alive she would walk a mile to see that we had cabbage.

On boy! You had to have cabbage on New Year's Day. That was just one of the ways she was raised up. So we took off that way, too. I don't think my son pays any attention to it. He's got no money anyway!

A Sign of Death

Ceil Schafer
talking to Beverly Kenoyer

Another thing they say — if a dog should howl three times, that's a sign of a death. If a train — if you're in a funeral procession and if the train should stop you, they said that there would be a death in a year.

Signs of Death

Thelma Long
talking to Jill DeSplinter

Don't rock an empty rocking chair. Grandma always said if you rocked an empty rocking chair it was the sign of death in the family.

Or there's a bird gets in the house. That was the sign that we're gonna have a death in the family.

The Way to Cross a Cat's Tracks

Murt Harrington
talking to J. R. Haskins

There's only one way that a person can cross a cat's track if there's no way to get around, and that is to turn your hat around, put the bill in the back, and then cross.

Good Luck for a Baby

Catherine Behm
talking to Kathy Smith

At the age of six, I remember so well when my brother was born. I was told to stay outdoors till the doctor came to bring us a new baby. The doctor came. I saw him with what they called then a satchel. I heard my mother crying so hard from the bedroom window I cried, too.

Finally the doctor came out and told me I could go in to see my baby brother. My father was holding him. I was the second to hold him.

An old neighbor lady came in and put a fifty-cent piece of money in his little hand. That was supposed to be very good luck.

Horsehair Snakes

Dales Sheets
talking to Shana Nesius

My mother had a few superstitions. One thing—to bring a hoe in the house is bad luck, and it would mean a death in the family if you brought a hoe in the house.

There's another one which I later found the reason for. It's not exactly a superstition; it's a misunderstanding of natural phenomenon. My dad used to believe that there were such things as horsehair snakes. He used to believe that if a long hair of a horse went into the creek, it would become a snake in the creek. And my father was very sure that it happened, because he had seen them. And I saw them, too, because these hairs just weave through water like a snake, and they move like a live animal. My brothers were going to night school and their agriculture teacher told them it wasn't so, that horses' hair didn't turn to snakes. What happen was that a lot of little animals, one-celled animals, grow on it, and they had this hair-like cilia

110

on it that would move the water. So you get enough of this one-celled animal on there, and it would look like a snake. My father still wouldn't accept that because you couldn't see them. It still looked like a snake to him.

Joint Snakes

Myrtle Dowell
talking to Brian Dowell

I heard about joint snakes when I was a kid. Mom, I think, was the one who told me about it, and it was hard to believe. Of course, as a kid you believe a lot of things. She called it a glass snake, and she said that if it was broken (I think the snake was supposed to do this, but you could do this yourself if you could catch the thing) the pieces could be put together and they would grow together.

Mistakes in Weaving

Lavonne Scheffe
talking to Teresa Brettnacher

When we warped a loom we added two extra warp threads. One extra thread was on the left. The reason it wasn't added on the right is because they believed that the right hand is God's hand. It won't err as easily as your left, so you add your extra thread on your left to help keep the salvage on the left straight. The Lord controls your right hand, and you're gonna keep that side straight.

The other extra thread, believe it or not, would be anywhere in the center of the rug, or placemat, or whatever you were weaving. The center thread is carried in just at random to let evil spirits and wickedness out of the rug, due to the fact that all things that are made of animals and are woven by hand may be touched by someone that doesn't share the faith, and, therefore, there would be evil in it.

Wedding Superstition

Eva Talley
*talking to Ellen Goad, Sally
Waymire, Roger Emond, Tony
Anderson, and Peggy Mormann*

I remember my father often had people come to the house
to be married, instead of having him go to their homes or
to the church. So a railroad fireman who was getting
married — my father had known from a little boy — came to
ask him if he would marry him a certain day. And he told
him he would. So my mother always tried to have some
cake and coffee and everything to serve after the wedding,
and she did. And we all got sort of dressed up in our best
clothes, and they came. And when they came in the man
told my father he'd like to talk to him a minute. So he said
that his wife thought it was a very bad thing for a bride and
groom to stand with the boards so there'd be a seam in the
floor between them. They wanted to stand the way the
boards ran in the floor. Well, my father asked my mother
if she knew which way the boards in the parlor ran. She
couldn't remember, so they had to take the carpet up in

Contributed by Mrs. Marvin Nussbaum

112

one corner. They had this Brussels carpet, and it was put down under the baseboards at the edge. But they took it up and found out which way the boards ran and got the couple stationed in the right direction, so they were married and lived happily ever afterwards.

Weatherlore, I

Ceil Schafer
talking to Beverly Kenoyer

If the corn husks are heavy, that's a sign of a cold winter. If the corn husks are light, it's a sign of a mild winter. This year, seemingly, they are lighter so maybe this year will be a milder winter.

Weatherlore, II

Mike Williams
talking to Mike Faker

I remember that my uncle, when he lived on the farm, would go by the hedge. If the leaves wasn't as big as squirrel ears, he'd say, "It's too early to plant corn. It's gonna get frosted." And my uncle used to say, "Sun set clear Friday night, rain before Monday night." Sundogs on each side of the sun meant a sign of storm warnings.

"Pill"

Dorothea Wolfe
talking to Dave Moseley

My husband's name was Lloyd, but no one actually called him that name. He was called "Pill." His mother used to sing a song, "You my, you my sweet little Pill." You know, a little song to put him asleep. And he had an older brother who could not say "Lloyd," and so he came up with the name Pill. Pill was my "sweet little Pill," and he went through school, high school, the whole bit, thirty years on the mail route, and he was known as Pill. And those who did not think it was Pill, thought it was "Phil."

The Boy Named "Boots"

Hershel Deardurff
talking to John Deardurff

When I was six year old, I was goin' to school right close to our home, and Dad bought me a little pair o' fleece lined boots, rubber boots. I wore them to school, and from there on they called me "Boots."

One night I was goin' home after a rain, and the boys told me to not go around by the road, to go through the field there and wade that corn for 'em. What they wanted is for me to get my boots full of water, and I sure did.

"Sod Pounder"

Carl Thompson
talking to Brad Thomas

Oh, my nickname was "Sod Pounder" because I walked heavy on my feet. It was given to me when I was a usher at the Colfax Theatre in South Bend, Indiana. The ushers claimed they could hear me escorting people to their seats. I would plod down the aisle, so I gained the nickname "Sod Pounder."

Contributed by Ellen Goad

The School Called "Never Fail"

Leona May
talking to Kam May

The school, where I lived on the farm, was called "Never Fail." My grandfather lived with us, and he was a Methodist preacher. He said that he always went to that schoolhouse *every* Sunday morning for Sunday school. Sometimes there was only one there, but he never failed. So they named the school "Never Fail."

Legend of the Maumee River

Sue Sutton
talking to Rhonda Sutton

We always asked about the Maumee River and how it got its name. And my mother use to tell us that there was a little Indian boy that got separated from its mother on the other side of the river and kept hollering "Mommy, Mommy," so, eventually, they just called it the Maumee River.

Vòdoo Crossing

Glenn Meadors
talking to Dave Phillips

Voodoo Crossing north of Reynolds. Several people got killed there. You come up and over it like that. Way up and high, and if you go over it very fast you just keep right on agoin'. You'll come down, zoom, like the Duke of Hazzard!

Monon's Early Name

Lydia McDonald
talking to Chris Annis

It's an Indian name. The original name is Monong and that was an Indian name meaning "running water." It originated as New Bradford; and when the railroad went through, the Monon Railroad, they changed the name of the town to Monon after the railroad.

An Early Name for Chalmers

Phillip Flora
talking to Dan Flora

Chalmers, the town that I was grown up in, originally was called Mud Station. All the territory west of there, which Wolcott would be included in, was heavy black dirt. No tiling or ditching had taken place at that time, and it was nothing but mud. It wasn't tilled or anything. And they'd run cattle in.

Seafield

Sam Kilgus
talking to Steve Hofstetter

I believe it [Seafield] was named because the Monon ditch that went through there was not as deep as it should have been. The water many times didn't get away, and things were flooded. I believe that is what give it the name Seafield.

Naming the Stops on the Mail Route

Russell Teeter
talking to Glen House

When my father got out of the Civil War they didn't have rural routes even in those years. They had what they called star routes. They didn't have many railroads. It was after the Civil War that most of the railroads were built. My grandfather lived close to Headlee and he'd ride down to Monticello and pick up mail, and he'd carry it back and deliver it to the country stores. He'd stay all night at home, and the next day he'd go to Winamac carrying the mail up there and delivering it to Pulaski, Bell Center, and some of them towns. He'd take the mail from Monticello to Winamac and leave it there, 'cause they had a railroad. He'd pick up mail to be delivered on the road back. He'd come back to home and stay all night, so he'd make the round trip from his home in Monticello all in one day.

A little interesting thing along that line was, my father, — I remembered him sayin' that the coldest place on the whole trip was after he'd cross the Tippecanoe River near Monticello and start north toward what now is Sitka. It was just a country store. That was the coldest place he was. He came near freezin' ridin' horseback with sacks of mail.

They used to just address "White County" for letters in this area, and they finally said you had to name the little stores and put that name to it. So he said to my father, and his sister just younger 'n him, he said, "You help name these stores." So father had heard about buyin' Alaska, and the first capital of Alaska was Sitka. Because Dad used to get so cold there, he said, "Let's name that little store Sitka." Aunt Abby used to get on the horse so their father wouldn't have to ride two extra miles. She'd take the mail up to Headlee, and because Headlee was the man's name that ran a grocery store there she said, "We shall name that store Headlee." So these two areas in White County has their names' sake by my father and my Aunt Abby.

Contributed by Louise Ward

People Passing By

There are probably as many itinerant people today as there were fifty years ago, but today people living on farms and in small towns are not as rooted as they once were. The stranger passing through is not as conspicuous. He comes down the interstate, stops at the local truck stop, and moves on with no one taking note. The dramatic distinction between native and alien, although still vestigially maintained in many small communities, has been eroded by the impervious flux of commerce. In these reflections our informants describe the peddlers, hucksters, tramps, and gypsies whose visits were isolated events met sometimes with apprehension, often with welcome.

Peddlers and Bottle Collectors

Irene Schmitz
talking to Tony Anderson

We had a lot of peddlers. We had people come along that sold, oh, maybe, they would sell a package of needles and needle threaders. Generally, it was small items that they could carry on the back in the pack. My mother usually bought needles whether she needed them or not. It was mostly that kind of thing. Maybe they would carry small pans, cooking pans, but nothing very large. Maybe a ladle, or a dipper, or something like that. She'd usually buy something, because she said, "I don't want to turn them down, because I know they probably need the money." A dime or whatever it was for each little thing. But she'd do that.

Then, also, we had people who came around that weren't peddlers, but they collected medicine bottles. When you used to get your medicine at the drug store, they would put it in a bottle with a label and a cork instead of a cap on it. Everybody kept their bottles, and you washed them out and maybe returned them to the drug store here in town. And they could be used again. Or if you took a bottle and cooked up a cough remedy or something, you would clean the bottle and take it back, and they would refill it for you. Or these peddlers would come along, and we would go around and hunt up bottles and wash them, and they generally had an old peddler's cart they called it. They carried all their old bottles and everything just piled up in there. I never could understand how they didn't get all broken, but I guess they didn't.

The German Visitor

Jane Packard
talking to Bryan Dunbar

One of them was a man who had come to the house one Monday morning, and our mother always washed on Monday morning. She had to heat water in the kitchen. This man showed up at the back door, and he indicated that he was hungry. She took time out from her washing to cook for him, and she cooked a big slice of ham. As I recall there was a dozen eggs. She put them in front of him. Also, she baked bread, and so he ate almost a whole loaf of home baked bread that morning. Since he didn't seem to have any other place to go, my father permitted him to stay on the farm. He didn't do very much work, but he did once in a while go out in the cornfield, in May or June, when he first came. He did go out in the cornfield and sometimes hoed. But he never did go out on any of the farm equipment. He stayed or slept, rather. My mother would not permit him to sleep in the house, so he slept in a loft over the garage part of the time, and then later he put some boards across a little place in the haymow over one of the grain bins and put some hay up there. That's where he slept all that summer.

One of his prized possessions seemed to be a leather coat that he wore. Even in the hottest days of July when he went to the field, that leather coat went with him everywhere. We children had rather fertile imaginations, and we used to wonder why he took the coat with him everywhere. Since he was German—As a matter of fact his accent was so very heavy, and it was very difficult to understand his English. Since that was true, we used to pretend that he was a spy and that he had some kind of papers sewn into the lining of his coat. But he did carry that leather—It was sort of a short leather jacket. He did carry that leather jacket everywhere. He did not leave it around anywhere. It was on a chair or hung up on a doorknob when he came into the house to eat. He was a rather strange person.

My mother almost always had fried chicken and gravy for Sunday dinner, and of course, when the strawberries were ripe we had strawberry shortcake. One Sunday, after the main part of the meal was over, the strawberry short-cake was passed to this man, and he would like to have some of that gravy, and he put chicken gravy on his strawberry shortcake. That gives you another idea of his peculiarities.

In the Ruins of the Glass Factory

George Scott
talking to Peggy Mormann

Well, I can't remember any ghost stories just off hand, but there was one story that terrorized the whole town of Fairmont for awhile when I was a little kid, about second or third grade. My part of the county had a gas boom, and there was just natural gas wells all over the place. I can remember the town of Fowlerton which, well, today it might have a hundred to a hundred-'n'-fifty people in it, had saloons along its main street. Boom type of deal like a wild western. And glass factories would spring up in these small towns, and when the gas wells dried up, well, the glass factories were left. I think there's only one left. This is where the Ball Brothers in Muncie got their start. And, besides Ball Brothers, the only other organization is a glass factory in Elwood that's still operating, but every other one, that I know of, is closed up. Course, by the time I was a kid the place was in ruins, where they had this glass factory, but there still were the little tunnels in underneath where the ovens were and some other part of the manufacturing apparatus (they had created tunnels and, course, it was a good place to play hide-'n'-seek for the kids).

But there was the one time someone had escaped from the insane asylum in Richmond, and was rumored to be in the Fairmont area and hiding in the glass factory. So all the kids carried little pocket knives to school, and they used these for protection. Course, the school was only a couple blocks from the glass factory. People used to sit up all night with shotguns hoping to protect their homes, the ones that lived close to the glass factory. It was quite a sensation for about a week, a week and a half, and then the story sort of evaporated. No one ever saw the guy, and he didn't attack anybody, so we don't really know if he was there. But the more adventurous kids used to gang up and go in there and try to see if they could find him. They could never find him.

Hucksters

Paul Clark
talking to Denise Strasburger

On the wagons they used to have a team of horses and a huckster man who would deliver kitchen stoves on wagons. They traveled through the country selling—I think "Majestic" was the name of the stoves, and their biggest advertisement was polished tops. The housewives wanted a stove so they could polish the tops and make them slick and shiny. And the Majestic Stove was one of those sold. Oh, seemed to me about in the 1930s this started. During the Depression they started traveling through the countryside selling these. I know my mom and dad, they bought one. I think they give $120 for a cook stove, coal burning stove. On one end you had a hot water jacket that you put, oh, it seemed to me like eight maybe ten gallons of water in, and you always had hot water from the heat of the stove.

And you had travelers who sold pots and pans. I can remember pots and pans by a man traveling through the country. He went through the country every so often, and he had cast iron pots and pans, and then there was another kind of a ware that they sold so foods wouldn't stick to it. They would sell you these in the same way as they did the stoves. They would sell you these and then deliver them two to three months later. They would sell these wares then ship them out to you. I can remember Dad had to go, and we picked up his stove. We had to go to Seafield. They had a depot. The stove came by train, shipped it to

Seafield, and Dad would go and pick it up. Same way with the pots and pans. I can't remember the name of the pots and pans, but they advertised that the food would not stick to the pan. But everytime I did it the stuff stuck.

In those days we also had people who delivered groceries. I did that myself—drove a huckster wagon for the People's Store in 1936. It delivered groceries to people in the country. We'd exchange eggs for groceries. Eggs would be twelve to fifteen cents a dozen. They would trade you so many dozen eggs for flour or sugar. They had crates for the hens and a carton for the eggs, and they would resell them to other customers on the way. Maybe the huckster would come to your place and you would sell five dozen eggs, go on and maybe someone else would want a dozen, so the eggs would be sold to someone else. Not chickens, chickens could not be resold. I think the reason for that was to keep down the disease in chickens. You couldn't take them from one farm to another. Mostly what people sold was an old roaster that was too old or a hen that wouldn't lay any longer. They'd keep the young ones for their own purpose.

I can remember when the first bakery-baked bread come from the bakery. Now they traveled through the country delivering bakery-baked bread. Now my mother always made homemade bread. She would make those great big loaves eight at a time or maybe twelve at a time. She put four in one pan and four more in the other pan. But this guy would come selling bakery bread, and us kids thought bakery bread was like angel food cake, it was a treat. So Mom would trade him four loaves of her home-made for a loaf of the bakery bread, and it was like angel food cake!

The Rum Runners

Glenn Meadors
talking to Dave Phillips

Before I got married, that was when they had the old rum running days through here. If you was in on the know—

126

They drove big old Packards, and they'd tear the back seat out and put five gallon cans in the back end and lay a blanket over them. They was completely flat across there. The springs sagged pretty heavy back there because of all that weight. Us younger fellows knew those fellows personally, when they came through here. We loafed down there at the service station, and they wanted to be friends with us. We could tip them off when somebody might be looking for them, and every once in a while they would be big hearted and give us a pop bottle full of alcohol, and we could have a mixed drink. From the service station to Montmorenci was twenty miles, and they'd sell a load of alcohol, or whatever you want to call it, in Chicago. Then another bunch would take off, and they'd know the make of that car and where it was going. They'd send some other fellows out, and they'd intercept him down here. They'd have runnin' gang wars down this road. There were no towns or anything along there. It was a runnin' gun battle down that road at times. I'm not kidding you — that's no bologna!

You didn't go out and butt in. You stayed out of it, and you'd be all right. They'd have runnin' and they'd steal that off of those fellows, take it away from them. Then they'd take it back to Chicago, and then they'd sell it again. That thing went on all the time through here. Us younger fellas, we knew those guys personally. When they'd come through they'd stop down there and want to know if we saw so and so. "Yeah, we saw him all right." "How long ago did he go through here?" "Oh, an hour and a half."

Gypsies

Irene Schmitz
talking to Tony Anderson

Oh, we had gypsies, and the funniest thing is they usually came to town about the middle of the afternoon. They hardly ever came in the morning, and they usually came from the east. Where they came from I don't know, but they usually came from the east and went on west. I don't know where they went, over into Illinois or something.

But one time we came home from school in the afternoon around three, and down by the old Mason's building, across the street where the filling station is now, we saw these gypsies standing around and saw these funny old little wagons all painted funny, you know, and real fancy. On the corner was a huge rock, and there was a gypsy woman sitting on there, and she had two or three little kids with her. They had on earrings, all kinds of bright blouses, full skirts, and that was the closest I ever got to what we would call a real gypsy.

Well, they went up and down Main Street to the business district, in and out of the stores, and oh, they were very sly. They would go into one store and they would want something in the back of the store or the front of the store, and another one of their bunch would come in while the clerk was waiting on the one in the back. The one in the front would pick up something and stick it in their clothing and walk back to the back of the store where the other one was and let on like he never done anything wrong. But after they left, the storekeeper could see the things that had been stolen. They did that nearly every place they went in. They were sly.

One time, I don't know what it was they stole, but anyway the storekeeper saw them take it, and he went to hunt the town marshall. I guess he didn't find him right away, and they started out west of town. I don't know how far they got out here, about two miles I think they said. But they caught up with these gypsies, and they were in horse and wagons, the horse carriage things. Well, whoever went after them had the old car, an old Ford, and they caught them west of town, and they got the ones. It was a woman and a man. I think they stole five dollars from one of the stores uptown, got it out of the cash register. But they got them.

The Uncanny

Stories of premonitions, mysterious lights, ghostly presences, and strange, half-human characters are the unfailing resources of almost anyone who has told or will tell a story. Whether such stories proceed from the need to explain or to invent the inexplicable, they have an enduring fascination for the young and old, the naive and the sophisticated.

Tokens

Marcella Kemp
talking to David Goy

Back in the olden days my mother used to talk about, they called them "tokens." You don't hear that word used anymore. It would be something that would happen before someone would die.

She had a relative, an elderly relative that was very ill, lived out in the country, and this relative was on her death bed. She said that her father told her that there was a sound at the door, and he went to the door, and there was no one there. It was a sound, he said, like someone had thrown a rock against the door. So he would open the door. This happened several times, and no one would ever be there. Finally, the last time there were pebbles all over the floor, the front porch floor, and he went outside and looked all around. There just wasn't a thing. And that time, when he went back into the house this person had died.

Somebody Called My Name

Mabel Griffin
talking to John Lemming

I think I was about eleven or twelve when my Uncle's children were drowned. On that very day that they drowned somebody said, "Mabel." I walked clear out to the chicken house to see if George or my father had called me. I looked around, but they had not called me. But I had been called! That seems strange. We didn't know until two or three days later when we got a telegram about it.

There were a lot of floods and rains. And they were backing up the car so they could turn around. And the creeks were all getting high and the swirl of this—it was called the Caterpiller River—the swirling water washed these children out of the car. After, Uncle John had to break glass for them to get out. So the three children were drowned, and she hung onto a tree and he swam to safety. Of course, he lost the use of three of his fingers from breaking the glass. He severed these ligaments that go into the fingers.

The Cemetery Light

Marcella Kemp
talking to David Goy

We had a cemetery in Noblesville, which is outside of Indianapolis which is where my husband is from. And he said they had a story there that one tombstone—You could drive by it at night and there'd be a light on it. And of course, all the young teenagers that were driving, that's where they'd go, to see the light at nighttime.

And there were wild stories that they had dug up the grave and found that the person had died of cancer, had taken a lot of radium treatments. And they tried to say that the radium was coming up through the ground causing the light. And this went on for years. My husband says everyone talks about it. And finally, somebody a little bit smarter than everybody else finally decided it was a reflection from a street light a half a block away.

Scare the Liver Outa You

Hershel Deardurff
talking to John Deardurff

We lived close to a cemetery, and us boys, after we'd break up at the school, would have a skatin' party over in the timber close to my home. We'd all walk and carry lanterns. Well, I'd go through the timber goin' to the party. Then I'd come home around the road, 'cause I was afraid of ghosts

131

and stuff. Well, I had to pass the cemetery just before I got home, and the moon was shinin' and I looked up to that cemetery expectin' to see a ghost. Sure enough I seen him! He was shinin' on that big polished cemetery tombstone. Likin' to scare the liver outa me.

The Man Who Didn't Believe in God

Marcella Kemp
talking to David Goy

My grandfather used to tell—Down there in Chillicothe, Ohio, there was a man who didn't believe in God. And he had made the statement that when he died he hoped that snakes just crawled all over him. And they claim to this day you can go to that grave and there's snakes there.

Contributed by Richard Wheeler

Buried Alive

Marcella Kemp
talking to David Goy

They tell a story — I think it was in Dayton, Ohio, back in the days when they had an epidemic of sleeping sickness. As you know, back in those days they couldn't embalm people, so you could really have sleeping sickness and give the appearance of being dead. They were supposed to have had a young girl there that they thought was dead, but she wasn't. She had sleeping sickness and was in an unconscious condition. They buried her.

And here, they said, on the front room window appears a ghostly picture of this girl, and it had a wreath around it. And they said that people came from all over to look at this picture on this window, the picture of this girl. And they dug up her grave, and when they dug it up they saw where she had clawed the sides of the casket trying to get out, and she had turned over.

Them's Dead Who Stays Dead

Herbert McGill
talking to Eric McGill

One time we's settin' up with a neighbor man. Well, he's a blacksmith was what he was — a pretty good size, husky guy. He died, and a whole bunch around there settin' up with him. About the middle of the night when we's all settin' around there half asleep, talkin' this and that, drinkin' wine and stuff, tryin' to keep awake, he raised up in the coffin. Another guy settin' there had a hammer there, and he went over and hit him on the head and he said, "Them's dead who stays dead." I guess it killed him then!

The Haunted Curve in the Road

Anonymous
talking to Tina Black

There was this road in West Virginia. It used to be straight. They built it straight when they built it, but then right in that one spot cars or trucks, either one, would be turned over. So they done some checkin'. They said the only thing that could cause it, they found out there was an ole Indian been buried there, and they'd built the road right over the grave. Well, then they put a curve, built out around it. They said that was the only thing that coulda been doin' it. They never had no turnin' over no more after they rounded out around it.

Ghost Hollow

Russell Teeter
talking to Glen House

When the Norway Dam was being built the people from Monticello liked to drive out and see how far along they was coming. They went through old "Ghost Hollow" we called it, north of our home. We had fun puttin' an old suitcase out on the road and see people stop and go pick it up. They didn't have four wheel brakes in them days — the old Model T was just one wheel brake — so by the time they got back to where the suitcase was, we pulled it over the edge of the hill. It was sort of fun to holler a little bit, and they'd jump in the car and away they'd go. Now that was the meanness that we did.

A Ghostly Presence

Dale Sheets
talking to Shana Nesius

I recall my dad telling, on different occasions, his experiences with a spirit that haunted a house he had visited a couple of times. One of his relatives lived there, and he had heard about this house for a long time. They always felt that someone had been murdered in the house and the ghost of this person came back to haunt this house. At any rate, he said he didn't believe this story at all. One winter night he was over there playing cards at the table, and he had to go to the door to throw out an apple core or something. He opened the screen door, and as his hand went out through the screen door something grabbed ahold of it very firmly—like another hand that reached out and grabbed it, held it for a moment, then let it loose. He came back in the house, and he was white! He then began to believe the story that was told about the house.

The woman that lived in the house told about coming down to fix breakfast in the morning before daylight, and she was suddenly aware that this ghost was standing behind her, beckoning to her. It didn't say anything, just stood there. She was frightened and started to run away, and the ghost disappeared.

But there are many stories about this old house that my dad said he didn't believe until that night when he put his hand out the screen door and something grabbed ahold of it.

The Haunted House

Mabel Griffin
talking to John Lemming

We used to have corn shuckers. When they used to shuck the corn by hand and throw it into the wagon, they had to have a peg in their hand to break open the husk with. They got up very early every morning, about four o'clock, and they tried to husk a hundred bushel of corn before ten o'clock. One always tried to outdo the other! Well, they would have their meal along about ten o'clock — that would be their noon meal. Even breakfast was potatoes and meat. They really ate a good meal so they could work like this.

There were many things they did in those days that one almost forgets. When you were young, you do almost forget these things. But I do remember they would get together (the guys) after they had worked that day, and they would tell each other stories — ghost stories. We kids were small, and we would listen.

The one that I think impressed us the most was: there was an old house — I think some of these men would come from Kentucky and Tennessee (the corn huskers that they would hire for the season to shuck the corn). They told about an old house, they called it haunted in those days. And they said they went into the house, and no matter how much they would put against this door, it was always pushed open. Come to find out, many years later they found out the history of the house, that someone had been killed there. There was also another person who had been kept there, and evidently they were retarded or something, and they would hear screams in the night. So, of course, that was very impressive to we kids to hear these things as they told the ghost story that said, "There's nobody here but you and me," and the other person said, "Pretty soon there won't be anybody but you, not me."

The House Built on the State Line

Helen Woolley
talking to Brian Molter

Well, we had a haunted house, or they said that we lived in a haunted house at one time. The house that we lived in was right on the state line. One half of the house was in Indiana, and one half was in Illinois. Of course, I was just a small child and didn't remember this, but I remember what my folks told me—that while they lived there, it wasn't very long, doors would open and slam just for unknown reasons, and so they moved out in two or three months' time.

The Ghostly Horses and Carriage

Dale Sheets
talking to Shana Nesius

People can imagine things, but dogs don't imagine things. So the reaction of dogs was one of the proofs they used to give for a ghost in a house—or that it was haunted.

One evening in this haunted house, there was a racket on the stairs leading down to the bedroom, and the door flew open and there were two white horses pulling a carriage behind. It came thundering down the steps or stairway, went over the bed, and out through the window. The dogs were so frightened, and barking, and ran under the bed. It was a ghost apparition that they couldn't explain. Both of them saw it, and the definitive thing about it was the fact that the dogs barked and ran under the bed. That house finally burned down. And my dad always wanted to go back and dig around the foundation of that house and see if there might be some bones buried under there, or some buried treasure.

Sleeping with the Rats

Anonymous
talking to Tina Black

My grandpap stayed all night with a guy. The guy told him, he said, "You're welcome to stay all night if you put up with the rats. You might not be able to sleep for the rats." He said the rats didn't bother him. Oh, he went outside before he went to bed and made three marks on the side of the house, and the guy never was bothered by rats no more. Said they had a big snow on. He went out the next morning, and he seen rat tracks aleavin' the barn, the house, and everything.

The World Was Coming to an End

Ruth Humphreys
talking to John Lemming

One winter—It must have been about 1917. It was during World War I. We had a Red Cross box social to make money for the Red Cross. Everybody was pretty hard up those days, and so we had this Red Cross social upstairs above what used to be Fowler's Implement Store. And when that was over, my friend, Dorothea Wolf, and I started home. We lived west of the schoolhouse here in Wolcott.

When we went downstairs we noticed that in the north the sky was red, and it just got redder and redder till it looked like it was going to burst into flames. We thought the world was coming to an end, and we were scared to death! We started running, and I fell in the ditch right in front of the schoolhouse and two of our classmate boys, that was doing just like boys do, kind of following us home, making cracks at us. We said, "Go on home. Can't you see the world's coming to an end, and get on home." We run on to Wolf's Store and fell up on, against, the door, and Mr. Wolf come to the door and see what was going on. He said, "What in the world is wrong?" And we said, "Oh, the world is coming to an end." I was thinking if I could just be out in Round Grove Township to my home when the world come to the end and be with my father and my brothers. We both got sick and threw up. We was that scared! But the world didn't come to an end. It was the northern lights or the—what they call the aurora borealis. But none of us had ever heard of 'em. And I've never seen 'em like that since.

138

Haunted House

Anonymous
talking to Tina Black

Well, they say that there was this house up there on Olive Hill — They'd give $1,000 for anybody who could go in the house.

A little boy lived with his grandmother there. Stayed there two weeks after his grandmother died, until someone seen him there and told them to go up there and get that kid because he was there by himself, and he was only about seven years old. Well, they went up there and got him. The sheriff, he couldn't go into the house. He had to talk the little kid into comin' outside. The sheriff said the glass all felt like it was comin' outa the house into his face when he started to walk in. Been several of them went up there and said you couldn't get in. Get as far as the porch, and it felt like the glass all in the house was flyin' out of it into your face.

The little boy said the grandmother put a curse on the house to protect him, I guess because he was so little, so nobody wouldn't come in on him. That's all I can tell you. They said they'd give $1,000 for anybody who could go in the house.

The Wild Boy

Geneva Spear
talking to Donna Pierson

Well, this isn't a ghost story if ghost stories are something false. Why, this is the truth. At one time people began complaining about missing eggs and chickens and little pigs from their farms. They kept seeing what they thought was a two-legged animal, and they'd shoot at it. Finally, one day someone hit it, and they captured it. This fella was born with features that weren't normal. He had a grotesque lookin' face, and his folks had died. He had just wandered into the country and was living in the woods. He'd pick berries and what have you in the summertime, and in the wintertime he was stealing chickens and whatever he could get from people's homes. Finally, when they caught him they nursed him back to health after he'd been shot, and one family took him in and kept him, and he worked for them.